ADMINISTRATION

AND

FINANCE

TRANSLATION:

FROM ENGLISH INTO ARABIC

الترجمة الإدارية والمالية:

من اللغة الإنجليزية الى اللغة العربية

Dr. Muhammad Ali Alkhuli

Publisher : DAR ALFALAH	الناشر: دار الناشر والتوزيع
P.O. Box 818	ص . ب 818
Swaileh 11910	صويلح 11910
Jordan	الأردن
Tel & Fax 0096266-5411547	هاتف وفاكس 009626-5411547
books@daralfalah.com E-mail:	
Website: www. daralfalah.com	

2008 Edition

الناشر: دار الفلاح للنشر والتوزيع	Publisher : DAR ALFALAH
ص. ب 818	P.O. Box 818
صويلح 11910	Swaileh 11910
الأردن	Jordan
هاتف وفاكس5411547 - 009626	Tel & Fax 0096266-5411547

رقم الإيداع دائرة المكتبية الوطنية
2001/9/1828

418, 022
Alkhuli, Muhammad Ali
Administration And Finance Translation:
From English into Arabic / Muhammad Ali Alkhuli
Amman: Dar Alfalah, 2001
(202) P
Deposit no: 1828/9/2001
Depositors: Translation / Business Management
* تم إعداد بيانات الفهرسة والتصنيف الأولية من قبل دائرة المكتبة الوطنية ، الأردن

رقم الاجازة المتسلسل لدى دائرة المطبوعات والنشر 2001/9/1749

ISBN 9957 - 401 - 43 - 2 (ردمك)

CONTENTS

بسم الله الرحمن الرحيم

PREFACE

مـقـدمـة

هذا الكتاب هو تدريب على الترجمة التجارية. والقطع فيه متنوعة من حيث محتواها، فهي في مجالات أربعة هي المحاسبة والأدارة العامة وإدارة الأعمال والعلوم المالية والمصرفية. والكتاب يحتوي على خمس وأربعين قطعة موزعة بالتساوي تقريبا على المجالات الأربعة سابقة الذكر. ولم أشأ أن أجعل عنوان الكتاب "الترجمة التجارية"، لأن مثل هذا العنوان مزدوج المعنى، لذا آثرت عنوان "الترجمة الأدارية والمالية ".

ويشمل الكتاب في بدايته جزءاً تمهيدياً يتناول المبادئ العامة في الترجمة. ويحسن بالأستاذ أن يوضح هذه المبادئ لطلابه قبل البدء بالترجمة. وبالطبع ، هناك مبادئ أخرى عديدة يمكن للأستاذ أن يوضحها لطلابه كلما رأى ذلك مناسباً.

ولقد جعلتُ عـدد الوحـدات خمسـاً وأربعـين وحـدة لتسـاوي عـدد المحاضرات في الفصل الدراسي الواحد، على أساس ثلاث محاضرات

أسبوعياً على مدى خمسة عشر أسبوعاً في الفصل الدراسي الواحد . هذا إذا افترضنا تدريس 45 محاضرة. وإذا كان عدد المحاضرات أقل ، فإن هذا يمكّن الأستاذ من اختيار ما يشاء من القطع واستثناء ما يشاء.

ومن أفضل الطرق لتدريس الترجمة – في رأيي – هي أن يقوم الطلاب بالترجمة المكتوبة خارج الصف، ثم يقوم الطلاب بتدقيق الترجمة بإشراف الأستاذ في أثناء المحاضرة ، ثم يقومون بكتابة الترجمة النهائية خارج الصف. بعبارة أخرى، هناك ثلاث مراحل: (1) كتابة الطلاب للترجمة الأولى في البيت، (2) تدقيق الترجمة بإشراف الأستاذ في الصف، (3) كتابة الطلاب للترجمة النهائية في البيت. لا شك أن هناك طرقاً أخرى لتدريس الترجمة، ولكنني أعتقد أن هذه الطريقة من أفضل الطرق. وعلى أي حال، يحسن بالأستاذ أن يجرب عدة طرق ويختار منها ما يروق له.

كل وحدة في الكتاب تحتوي على نص من صفحتين، وهي كمية كافية في الغالب لملء ساعة من الزمن هي وقت المحاضرة. وفي الحقيقة، قد لا يتمكن الأستاذ من ترجمة الصفحتين تحت ضغط الوقت . إن الأمر يتوقف على صعوبة النص وعلى مستوى الطلاب ومدى تحضيرهم وعلى طريقة تدريس الترجمة . لا شيء يلزم الأستاذ بترجمة الصفحتين ، إذ قد يكتفي ببعض الفقرات أو إحدى الصفحتين. ولكن هناك مجال مفتوح للطالب دائماً أن يترجم أكثر ما يستطيع من النص لأن لديه مجالاً أوسع من الوقت خارج الصف مما هو الحال في الصف تحت ضغط الوقت المحدود للمحاضرة.

بالإضافة الى النص ، تحتوي كـل وحـدة عـلى كلمـات مساعدة Helpful Vocabulary . وتظهر تحت هذا العنوان أهم العبارات الواردة في النص ، وتظهر أمام كل عبارة ترجمتها باللغـة الهـدف حسبما يتطلب السـياق ، وهي عبارات اصطلاحية في الغالب. هذه الصفحة مـن الكلمـات المسـاعدة لا تحتوي عـلى كـل المفردات والعبارات التي يحتاجها الطالب المترجم ، بل تحتوي عـلى أبرزهـا فقـط . وعلى الطالب أن يستعين بالمعجم كلما رأى ذلك ضروريا .

إضافة الى النص باللغة المصدر والكلمات المساعدة ، تحتـوي كل يوم وحـدة على تمرين لغوي ذي صلة بالنص. وأشيع هذه التمارين هنا هـو تمـرين الاشتقاق، حيث تظهر عـدة كلمات وردثْ في الـنص. وهـي مصنفة الى أفعـال أو أسـماء أو صفات، وعلى الطالب أن يشتق النوعين الآخرين. مـثلاً، إذا كانت الكلمـة فعلاً، فعليه أن يشتق منها الاسم والصفة . وإذا كانت صفة، فعليه أن يشتق منها الفعل والاسـم، وهكذا . وعليه أيضا أن يكتـب المقابل باللغـة الأخرى أمـام كـل كلمـة . والغاية من هذا التمرين إثراء حصيلة الطالب المفرداتية التي هي عامل أسـاسي في القدرة الترجمية .

وبما أن النصوص مقتبسة من كتب أو مجلات متنوعة ، فلقد ظهرت في آخر الكتاب قائمة تبين مصادر هذه الاقتباسات .

وختاماً ، أرجو أن يكون هذا الكتاب ذا فائدة لطلاب الترجمة ولكل من له اهتمام بالترجمة .

والحمدلله رب العالمين .

أ.د. محمد علي الخولي

7

GENERAL PRINCIPLES OF

TRANSLATION

مبادئ عامة في الترجمة

في بداية هذا الكتاب ، يحس تعريف الطالب بأهم المبادئ التي يجب أن تراعي في أثناء عملية الترجمة . ومن هذه المبادئ ما يلي:

1. إذا كانت الجملة في اللغة المصدر Source language غامضة المعنى (أي متعددة المعاني لسبب نحوي أو سبب مفرادتي) ، فعلى المترجم أن يحاول إزالة غموضها في اللغة الهدف target language كلما أمكنه ذالك.

2. يستحسن أن ينقل المترجم التأثير الذي قصده الكاتب في اللغة المصدر إذا كان المترجم مدركاً لذلك التأثير. هل كان الكاتب ساخطاً أم ساخراً أم هازئاً أم غاضباً أم منفعلاً ...الخ ؟ وهذا لا يتأتى إلا بالممارسة والخبرة والدراية باللغتين (اللغة المصدر واللغة الهدف).

3. لابد للمترجم من أن يفهم النص تماماً كشرط مسبق للبدء بالترجمة، إذ لا فائدة من ترجمة مبنية على سوء فهم النص .

4. على المترجم أن يتقيد بالمصطلحات المستخدمة في اللغة الهدف. وتزداد أهمية هذا المبداء في الترجمة التخصصية ، أي ترجمة النصوص

المتخصصة في العلوم أو القانون أو سواها من فروع المعرفة. هنا لا يفيد اختراع مصطللحات جديدة ، بل لا بد من الالتزام بالمصطلحات الشائعة في اللغة الهدف لتحقيق التفاهم اللغوي المنشود.

5. الأصل في الترجمة هو التقيد بنص المصدر ، وهذا ما يدعى الترجمة الحرفية. وإذا تعذر ذلك لسبب ما ، فعلى المترجم أن يتحول الى ترجمة المعنى.

6. على المترجم الالتزام بترجمة ثابتة لمصطلح ما ، فإذا ترجم المترجم المصطلح س بالمقابل ص في جملة ما في نص ما ، فعليه أن يستخدم ص مقابل س كلما ظهرت س في اللغة المصدر من أجل تحقيق مبادئ الوضوح والثبات والاتساق consistency.

7. العدد الرقمي (مثلاً 3000) يترجم بعدد رقمي (3000). العدد الكتابي يترجم بعدد كتابي ، مثلاً three hundred تترجم بـ ثلاث مئة.

8. في بعض الحالات، المصطلح يبقى كما هو . مثلاً ،phoneme يمكن أن تبقى كما هي(فونيم)fax، تبقى(فاكس).

9. الكلمة أو العبارة البارزة في اللغة المصدر يحافظ على بروزها في اللغة الهدف بطريقة مناسبة . مثلاً ، الكلمات المائلة أو المكتوبة بحرف أسود في اللغة المصدر يمكن إبرازها بالطريقة ذاتها أو بوضع خط تحتها في اللغة الهدف . عنوان الكتاب المكتوب بحرف مائل في اللغة الأنجليزية يترجم ألى العربية ويوضع تحته خط أو يطبع بحرف مائل.

10. قبل البدء بترجمة أول جملة في النص ، من الأفضل أن يقرأ المترجم النص كله كي يأخذ فكرة عامة عن الموضوع مما يسهل عليه ترجمة أجزائه .

11. كلمات النص نوعان: كلمات محتوى content word وكلمات وظيفة function word. على المترجم أن يترجم كلمات المحتوى ، ولكن ليس مطلوباً منه أن يترجم الكلمات الوظيفية ترجمة مباشرة دائماً لأن دور الكلمات الوظيفية يختلف عن دور كلمات المحتوى. ومن أمثلة الكلمات الوظيفية the, a, an, to .

12. إذا أراد المترجم إضافة كلمة من عنده إلى النص الأصلي فعليه أن يضعها بين قوسين هكذا[ ]. مثلاً ، هناك أنواع عديدة [من البكتيريا] تعيش في جسم الأنسان. الإضافة التي بين قوسين يضيفها المترجم من أجل مزيد من التوضيح أو لإزالة الغموض حسبما يرى المترجم الأمر ضرورياً .

13. إذا أراد المترجم توضيح النص بإضافة طويلة أو التعليق على النص، فعليه أن يضيف ملاحظة هامشية footnote و ألّا يضيف ذلك داخل النص ذاته . الإضافة داخل النص ذاته بين قوسين [ ] تقتصر على إضافة محدودة جداً لا تزيد عن كلمة أو اثنتين .

14. إذا كانت في اللغة الهدف عدة مقلبلات لمصطلح ما في اللغة المصدر، تعطي الأفضلية للأشيع أو الأدقّ منها.

15. بعد الترجمة الأولية ، على المترجم أن يراجع النص للتأكد من سلامته من حيث النحو والإملاء والترقيم ولتخليص النص من أية ركاكة أسلوبية محتملة .

16. لا يجوز للمترجم أن يخترع من عنده اختصارات (كلمات أوائلية) acronyms غير مألوفة لأن ذلك يعيق الاتصال بين المترجم والقارئ. ولكن يجوز للمترجم في حالات محدودة أن يستحدث اختصار بعد توضيحه اقتصاداً في التعبير إذا تكرر ظهور المصطلح عدة مرات ، مثلاً م ج ع (ميثاق الجامعة العربية).

17. إذا ظهرت كلمات أوائلية في اللغة المصدر ، فعلى المترجم أن يحولها إلى كلمات تامة في اللغة الهدف . مثلاً ، VIP تترجم إلى شخص مهم جداً) ، NATO تترجم إلى (منظمة معاهدة شمال الأطلسي) . وإذا كان الاختصار شائعاً جداً(مثل AIDS)، فلا داعي لترجمة ، بل يمكن أن يبقى كما هو في اللغة المصدر (أي الايدز) . ويجوز في بعض الحالات الجمع بين الاختصار وترجمه، مثل النيتو(منظمة معاهدة شمال الأطلسي).

18. يحافظ المترجم على حدود الفقرات وعددها . أي تبدأ الفقرة في اللغة الهدف مع بداية الفقرة في اللغة المصدر و تنتهي مع نهايتها . وبذلك، تتطابق الفقرات في اللغة المصدر واللغة الهدف من حيث البداية والنهاية والعدد.

19. من حيث الترقيم الخارجي، يجب أن يتطابق النصان (في اللغة المصدر واللغة الهدف) في ترقيم أواخر الجمل . النقطة تبقى نقطة ، وكذلك علامة الاستفهام وعلامة التعجب وعلامات الاقتباس والفاصلة المنقوطة ، مع فروق طفيفة في شكل العلامة أحياناً . مثلاً ، في اللغة الإنجليزية نستعمل ؟ و ؛ وفي العربية نستعمل ؟ و ؛ . لاحظ أن المقصود بالترقيم الخارجي هو الترقيم في نهاية الجملة.

20. من حيث الترقيم الداخلي (أي الترقيم داخل الجملة وليس في نهايتها) ، قد تختلف اللغات في أحكام هذا الترقيم . مثلاً ، استخدام الفاصلة في اللغة العربية لا يتطابق مع استخدامها في اللغة العربية لا يطابق مع استخدامها في اللغة الأنجليزية.

21. من حيث ترقيم الكلام المباشر ، نستخدم النقطتين في العربية والفاصلة في الأنجليزية . مثلاً ، قال : " ." . "," He said . كما أن اتجاه علامات الافتباس الفاتحة يختلف في اللغتين: نبدأ بــ ،، في الانجليزية، ولكن نبدأ بــ " في العربية. وكذلك تختلف علامات الاقتباس الخاتمة .

22. في العادة، الاسم العَلَــم لا يترجم . مثلاً مُحمد تبقى Muhammad ولا يجوز ترجمتها إلى the praised ، peter تصبح بيترأو بطرس وليس (الصخرة) . أما إذا كان العلم اسماً جغرافيا مركباً فالأشيع ترجمته . مثلاً، The Pacific Ocean تصبح (المحيط الهادي) ، the Red Sea تصبح (البحر الأحمر).

23. على المترجم أن يرجع إلى المعاجم المتخصصة إذا كان يترجم نصاً متخصصاً ، مثلاً ، نصاً طبياً أو هندسياً أو قانونياً ، لأن المعاجم العامة في العادة لا تسعفه في الترجمة التخصصة . المعجم العام يفيد في ترجمة النصوص العامة . وهناك معاجم متخصصة في شتى فروع العلوم والمعارف. هناك معاجم متخصصة عربية إنجليزية و إنجليزية عربية في الفيزياء والرياضيات والكيمياء والأحياء والتربية وعلم النفس والفلسفة وعلــم اللغة والمحاسبة والأدارة والقانون والسياسة والحاسوب وكل فروع العلم ، بل أن هناك معاجم متخصصة في فروع الفروع ، من مثل علم اللغة النظري وعلم اللغة التطبيقي وعلم الأصوات .

24. على المترجم ان يتحرى الدقة في الترجمة وخاصة في ترجمة المصطلحات المتقاربة ، أي المصطلحات التي يتقارب معناها دون أن يتطابق

25. على المترجم ألا يخمن معنى كلمة لايعرفها دون الرجوع الى المعجم، ألا اذا كان في موقف ترجمة فورية أو ترجمة تتابعية . في هذه الحالة، لا يوجد خيار آخر أمامه سوى خيار التخمين . ولكن أذا كان في موقف ترجمة كتابية ، فلا عذر له إذا لم يرجع ألى المعجم للتثبت من المعنى.

26. المعاني في أية لغة أكثر من الكلمات، ولذلك يندر أن نجد كلمة ذات معنى واحد. معظم الكلمات متعددة المعاني. ومن واجب المترجم أن يفهم المعنى المقصود في اللغة المصدر كي يختار ما يقابله في اللغة الهدف. وهذا هو التحدي الأكبر في عملية الترجمة : فهم النص في اللغة المصدر وإنشاء نص مقابل في اللغة الهدف.

27. الترجمة الكاملة ممكنة أحياناً ، ولكن الترجمة المُرضية ممكنة دائماً ، إلاَ أنها تتطلب الدقة والدراية والخبرة .

28. النثر يترجم إلى نثر. أما الشعر فيجوز أن يترجم إلى شعر إن أمكن أو إلى نثر إذا تعذرت ترجمتة الى شعر.

29. يتوجب على المترجم أن يتقن اللغتين : اللغة المصدر واللغة الهدف. يتقن الأولى ليفهم النص ويتقن الثانية ليكتب بها . ومن الواضح أن عدم الأتقان للأولى سيجعل الفهم مختلاً وأن عدم الأتقان للثانية سيجعل الكتابة مليئة بالأخطاء من كل نوع . وتصل الأمور إلى حد الكارثة إذا كان المترجم ضعيفاً في اللغتين : هنا تنشأ أخطاء عديدة في فهم اللغة المصدر وأخطاء عديدة في التعبير باللغة الهدف.

30. في الترجمة المتخصصة ، مثل الترجمة الطبية والهندسية ، يكون المترجم في وضع أفضل إذا كان عارفاً بالحقل الذي يترجم فيه ، بالإضافة إلى إتقانه للغتين بطبيعة الحال. ويمكن أن ندعو المعرفة بالحقل المعرفة التخصصية وأن ندعو معرفة اللغتين المعرفة اللغوية. ومن الواضح أن المعرفة التخصصية لا تغني عن المعرفة اللغوية ، فالمعرفة الطبية ، مثلاً ، لا تجعل الطبيب مترجماً . ولكن ، قد تغني المعرفة اللغوية عن المعرفة التخصصية، إذا يستطيع المترجم أن يترجم نصاً طبياً دون أن يكون

متخصصاً في الطب. ولا شك أن خير المترجمين من كانت تتوفر لديه المعرفة التخصصية والمعرفة اللغوية معاً ، ولكن قليلاً بل نادراً ما يتوفر مثل هؤلاء المترجمين .

31. إن عملية الترجمة عملية اتخاذ قرارات في كل لحظة ، إذ لا بد أن يتخذ المترجم قراراً عند ترجمة كل تركيب . وبالطبع ، حسن اتخاذ القرار يعتمد أساساً على المقدرة اللغوية للمترجم وعلى درايته بفن الترجمة أو علم الترجمة . كما أن عملية الترجمة - في العديد من المواقف - عمليت تستدعي إعادة المحاولة ، أي الترجمة ألى الأمام ثم العودة إلى الخلف ثم الى الأمام ، حتى يحس المترجم أن المنتوج قد استوى واستقرّ وأصبح مُرْضياً من حيث المعنى والمبنى .

32. للطالب العربي ، الترجمة من الإنجليزية إلى العربية أسهل بكثير من الترجمة من العربية إلى الإنجليزية، لأن الترجمة من الإنجليزية تستدعي فهم الإنجليزية والتعبير بالعربية ، ولكن الترجمة من العربية تستدعي فهم العربية والتعبير بالإنجليزية . صعوبة الأولى فهم الإنجليزية، أما صعوبة الثانية فهي التعبير بالإنجليزية. ولا شك أن التعبير أصعب من الفهم، فـي أغلب الأحيان.

UNIT 1

PUBLIC ADMINISTRATION:
WHAT IT MEANS

Administration refers to *mobilisation of resources* – human and material – to achieve pre-set objectives. Administration is, thus, an activity undertaken in pursuit of realisation of some goal. It is goal-oriented and purposive. It is, thus, a group effort requiring a group of persons, each individually carrying out certain allotted tasks, which, when so performed by all, lead to the achievement of a goal which has already been established and made explicit. Administration is a distinct activity in itself separate from **technical functions** being carried out. This may be illustrated.

The Kumbha Mela, as most of us know, is a big event in India. Once in a given number of years, more than a crore of devout Hindus congregate on the appointed days on the appointed days on the bank of devout Hindus congregate on the appointed days on the bank of the sacred river Ganga at Allahabad to take a dip in its holy waters. As people come from all parts of the country, arrangements for carrying them to and fro are necessarily to be made. Even special trains are run for the purpose. New townships equipped with all minimum activities are temporarily built to accommodate the pilgrims. Medical facilities are arranged. Roads are constructed, electricity is provided. Food supplies are arranged. Law and order are maintained. What is conveyed is that lakhs of public functionaries are employed almost overnight to perform, individually and separately, these myriad tasks. These numerous people work in an ordered way to ensure the successful holding of the Kumbha Mela. They work under the supervision, direction, and control of especially designated persons.

Those engaged in **supervision** and control are separate from those who construct roads, give medicines, transport pilgrims. They run the administration, and, thus, constitute a separate category whose task is to plan, supervise, control, and coordinate so that the given goal is accomplished. Administration is, thus, distinct from technical activity even though it is itself a specialisation, requiring possession of special skills. Administration deals with processes – like planning, organising, staffing, directing, coordinating, communicating, budgeting, and evaluating. It is by effective invoking of these several processes that things get done. *Dictionary of Administration and Management* edited by Ivan S. Panki (published by Systems Research, Los Angeles, 1981) defines administration as the sum of all the ideas, technologies, procedures and processes which are employed to help an organization maintain, control, and coordinate formally and informally organised human and material resources for achieving its *Predetermined goals*. Public administration is part, even though a large and important part, of administration. Administration means performance of the executive function of the state.

Helpful vocabulary:

public administration	إدارة عامة
mobilisation of resources	تعبئة الموارد
pre-set objectives	أهداف محددة مسبقاً
in pursuit of	من أجل
allotted tasks	أعمال مخصصة
to accommodate the pilgrims	يستوعب الحجاج
staffing	توظيف
procedures and processes	إجراءات و عمليات
executive function	وظيفة تنفيذية
the executive	السلطة التنفيذية
the legislature	السلطة التشريعية
the judiciary	السلطة القضائية
broadest sense	المعنى الأوسع
conduct of governmental affairs	تصريف الشؤون الحكومية
operation	تسيير
administrative sector	قطاع إداري
purposive	هادف
carry out	ينفِّذ
bank of the river	ضفة النهر
are run for	تُسيَّر من أجل
medical facilities	تسهيلات طبية
supervision and control	الإشراف و السيطرة

Exercise 1. *Translate the previous passage into Arabic.*

Exercise 2. *Fill in this table with the suitable English derivatives whenever possible, and write down the Arabic equivalents of all the words.*

Verb		Noun		Adjective	
English	**Arabic**	**English**	**Arabic**	**English**	**Arabic**
achieve					
		mobilisation			
				individual	
require					
				distance	
illustrate					
				technical	
arrange					
		purpose			
				sacred	
employ					
				necessary	
		supervision			
				devout	
accomplish					
		person			
		control			
				separate	

Exercise 3. *Translate these pairs:*

sources, resources   —————   construct reconstruct   —————

objective, subjective   —————   formal, informal   —————

react, interact   —————   extend ,intend   —————

demand, supply   —————   advise, advice   —————

monitory, monetary   —————   stationary, stationery   —————

UNIT 2

COMPARISON IN THE STUDY OF PIBLUIC ADMINISTRATION

Public administrations as an aspect of governmental activity has existed as long as political systems have been functioning and trying to achieve program objectives set by the political decision-makers. Public administration as a field of systematic study is much more recent. Advisers to rulers and commentators on the workings government have recorded their observations from time to time in sources as varied as kaustlya's *Arthasastra* in ancient India, the *Bible*, Aristotle's *Politics* and Machiavelli's *The prince* , but it was not until the eighteenth century that cameralism, concerned with the systematic management of **governmental affairs**, became a specialty of German scholars in western Europe . In the United States, such a development did not take place until the latter part of the nineteenth century, with the publication in 1887 of the Woodrow Wilson's famous essay, "The Study of Administration," generally considered the starting point. Since that time, public administration has become a Well- recognized area of specialized interest, either as a subfield of political science or as an academic discipline in its own right.

Despite several decades of development, consensus about the

scope of public administration is still lacking, and the field has been described as featuring heterodoxy rather than orthodoxy. A current text reviews the **intellectual development** of the field under the heading of public administration's " ninety years in a quandary." This may be strength rather than a weakness, but such a feature does rule out a short, precise, and generally acceptable definition of the field. The identification of the tendencies and of shared subject of concern is more feasible, and it is all that is necessary for our purpose.

public administration is presumably an aspect of a more generic concept - administration, the essence of which has been described as "determined action taken in pursuit of conscious purpose." Most efforts to define administration in general add the element of cooperation among two or more individuals and view it as cooperative human effort toward reaching some goal or goals accepted by those engaged in the endeavor. Administration is concerned with means for the achievement of prescribed ends. Administrative activity can take place in a variety of settings, provided the crucial elements are present: the cooperation of human beings to perform tasks that have been mutually accepted as worthy of the joint effort. The *institutional framework* in which administration occurs may be as diverse as a business firm, labor union, church, educational institution, or governmental unit .

Helpful vocabulary:

as long as	ما دام
program objectives	أهداف البرنامج
decision-makers	صُناع القرار, صانعو القرار
advisers to rulers	مستشارو الحكام
systematic management	إدارة منتظمة
with the publication	مع نشر
in its own right	مستقل
consensus about	الاجتماع بشأن
rule out	يستثني
educational institution	مؤسسة تربوية
public policy decisions	قرارات السياسة العامة
private administration	إدارة خاصة
identification of tendencies	تحديد الاتجاهات
range	مدى
dividing line	خط فاصل
subfield	حقل فرعي
somewhat narrowed	ضيق إلى حد ما
to signify	يدل على
unduly restrictive	مقيد دون داعٍ
sharp dichotomy	انقسام ثنائي حاد
influential book	كتاب ذو أثر، كتاب بارز
policy execution	تنفيذ السياسات
policy making	صُنْع السياسات، رسم السياسات
effective performance	أداء فعَّال
institutional framework	إطار مؤسسي

Exercise 1. *Translate the previous passage into Arabic.*

Exercise 2. *Fill in this table with the suitable English derivatives whenever possible, and write down the Arabic equivalents of all the words.*

Verb		Noun		Adjective	
English	**Arabic**	**English**	**Arabic**	**English**	**Arabic**
act					
		program			
advise					
		Europe			
				acceptable	
describe					
		America			
		public			
				current	
		heterodoxy			
				strong	
achieve					
		orthodoxy			
				famous	
range					
		politics			
				various	
occur					

Exercise 3. *Translate these terms:*

absentee landlord	_____	absolute monopoly	_____
absentee owner	_____	absentee sale	_____
absolute contract	_____	accepted bill	_____
absentee gift	_____	accident insurance	_____
service credit	_____	shipping charges	_____

UNIT 3

WHAT IS PUBLIC ADMINISTRAITON?

Let us give a moment's attention to a traditional dispute in the definition of *public administration*, and a related source of frequent confusion in the use of the term. The conflict has concerned whether public administration is an art or science. Some students and administrators, impressed with the achievements of the natural and physical sciences, have been insistent that public administration can and should become a science in the same sense .Other students and administrators, impressed with a fluid, creative quality in actual administration, with such intangibles as judgment and leadership, have been equally insistent that public administration cannot become a science, that it is an art

Much nonsense has resulted from the debates of the *science-art controversy* but also considerable clarification of concepts and agreement on usage. It is fashionable nowadays to refer to the "*art and science*" of public administration, in the manner of the second definition above. This usage reflects a general conclusion that public administration has important aspects of both science and art. It reflects also, however, a desire to bypass the definitional problems, to compromise the issue, by yielding to both sides .to get on with the study and practice of public administration, whatever it is. This disposition to get on is no doubt healthy, and diminishes a picayune and wasteful squabbling over words alone. But it must not be forgotten that definitions are important to fruitful study and effective action. The problem of how people are to be educated or trained for participating in public administration, for example, is one that can be solved only after a decision as to what, after all, is meant by public administration.

A fertile source of confusion and error , closely related to the science-art controversy, is the fact that the words "public administration" have tow usages. They are used to designate and delineate both (1) an area of *intellectual inquiry*, a designate or study, and (2) a process or activity - that of administering public affairs. While the tow meanings are of course closely related, they are nevertheless different, it is a difference similar to that between biology as the study of organisms and the organisms themselves.

Now if this distinction seems so obvious as not to warrant the making, the excuse must be that it is, nevertheless, a distinction often missed. It is obvious, in retrospect, that a great deal (but not all) of the controversy over whether public administration is a science or an art stemmed from failure to agree on which public administration was being discussed, the discipline or the activity.

Helpful vocabulary:

a moment's attention	لحظة انتباه
impressed with	معجب بـ
can and should	يستطيع و ينبغي
insistent that	مُصِرّ على أن
science – art controversy	جدلية العلم و الفن
definitional problems	مشكلات التعريف
to compromise the issues	يتوصل إلى حل وسط
to make the case for	يدافع عن
abruptly or gradually	فجأة أو بالتدريج
sometimes too	أحياناً أيضاً
clear intent	مقصد واضح
in the case of	في حالة
on the other hand	من ناحية أخرى
filing system	نظام الملفات , نظام الإضبار
distribution of work	توزيع العمل
employee morale	معنويات الموظفين
file clerk	موظف الملفَّات
minimum loss	خسارةٌ دنيا , الحد الأدنى من الخسارة
be content with	قانع بـ , راضٍ بـ
for the moment	حالياً , مؤقتاً
relating means to ends	ربط الوسائل بالأهداف
by definition	بحكم التعريف
to maximize realization of goals	لتحقيق الحد الأعلى من الأهداف
goal awareness	إدراك الأهداف
in the sense that	بمعنى أن

Exercise 1. *Translate the passage into Arabic.*

Exercise 2. *Fill in this table with the suitable English derivatives whenever possible, and write down the Arabic equivalents of all the words.*

Verb		Noun		13	
English	**Arabic**	**English**	**Arabic**	**English**	**Arabic**
		attention			
impress					
		dispute			
conclude					
		judgment			
				apparent	
compromise					
		debate			
educate					
		distinction			
				general	
designate					
		organism			
				close	
cultivate					
		stem			
discuss					
		discipline			
				confused	
		inquiry			
yield					

Exercise 3. *Translate these terms:*

accident rate	——————	account day	————
accommodation bill	——————	accounting concepts	————
account book	——————	accounting cycle	————
account balance	——————	accounting department	————
shipping document	——————	ship broker	————

UNIT 4

NATURE AND KINDS OF
CONTRACTS

The *law of contract* is the foundation upon which the superstructure of modern business is built. It is common knowledge that in business transactions quite often promises are made at one time and the performance follows later. In such a situation, if either of the parties were free to go back on its promise without incurring any liability , there would be endless complications, and it would be impossible to carry on trade and commerce . Hence, the law of contract was enacted which lays down the legal rules relating to promises: their formation, their performance and their **enforceability.** Explaining the object of the law of contract, Sir William Anson observes: "The law of contract is intended to ensure that what a man has been led to expect shall come to pass; that what has been promised to him shall be performed ."

The law of contract is applicable not only to the business community, but also to others. Everyone of us enters into a number of contracts almost every day , and most of the time we do so without even realising what we are doing from the point of law. A person seldom realises that when he entrusts his scooter to the mechanic for repairs, he is entering into a *contract of bailment*; or when he buys a packet of cigarettes , he is making a contract of the sale of goods; or again when he goes to the cinema to see a movie , he is making yet another contract; and so on.

Besides, the law of contract furnishes the basis for the other branches of *Mercantile Law*. The enactments relating to sale of goods, negotiable instruments,insurance,partnership, and insolvency are all founded upon the general principles of contract law. That is why the study of the law of contract precedes the study of all other sub-divisions of Mercantile Law.

The law of contract in India is contained in the Indian Contract Act, 1872. This Act is based mainly on English Common Law which is to a large extent made up of *judicial precedents*. It extends to the whole of India except the State of Jammu and Kashmir and came into force on the first day of September 1872. The Act is not exhaustive. It does not deal with all the branches of the law of contract. There are separate Acts which deal with contracts relating to negotiable instruments, **transfer of property,** sale of goods, partnership, insurance, etc. Again the Act does not affect any usage or custom of trade (Sec.1).

Helpful vocabulary:

law of contract	قانون العقود
business transactions	معاملات تجارية
incurring liability	تحمل المسؤولية
legal rules	أحكام قانونية
not only … but also	ليس فقط...ولكن أيضاً
mercantile law	قانون تجاري
either of the parties	أحد الطرفَيْن
go back on the promise	ينكث بوعده
come to pass	يُنَفَّذ
English Common Law	القانون الإنجليزي العام
to a large extent	إلى حد كبير
sale of goods	بيع السلع
transfer of property	نقل المِلْكية
to pass an act	يَسِنَّ القانون
assumptions underlying the act	افتراضات خلف القانون
contracting parties	الطرفان المتعاقدان
valid contract	عقدٌ سارٍ
rights and obligations	حقوق و التزامات
essential of the contract	أساسيات العقد
in absence of anything to the contrary	في غياب ما يفيد عكس ذلك
to give rise to	يؤدي إلى
enforceable by law	نافذ بموجب القانون
non-fulfillment of promises	عدم الوفاء بالوعد
plaintiff	مُدَّعٍ
defendant	مُدَّعَى عليه

Exercise 1. *Translate the previous passage into Arabic.*

Exercise 2. *Fill in this table with the suitable English derivatives whenever possible, and write down the Arabic equivalents of all the words.*

Verb		Noun		Adjective	
English	**Arabic**	**English**	**Arabic**	**English**	**Arabic**
		knowledge			
follow					
		foundation			
				free	
		promise			
				endless	
		complication			
				absolute	
incur					
		commerce			
enact					
		rule			
explain					
		repair			
intend					
		partner			
perform					
enter					

Exercise 3. *Translate these terms:*

accounting machines   ———————   accounting period   ———————

accounting methods   ———————   accounting report   ———————

accounting models   ———————   accounting statement   ———————

accounting office   ———————   accounting system   ———————

sub-contract   ———————   sub- contractor   ———————

UNIT 5

PUBLIC MANAGENT SYSTEMS

Public management systems are comprised of sets of public management actions that interact to form distinguishable effects on the community or populace they serve. These are always "open" systems since corrections to these systems must be effected by decisions made outside the systems, almost invariably human decisions. For instance, results are often interpreted differently by various public interest groups, thereby making meaningful measurement of results difficult. Unique human decisions are often mead to " correct" the system so that results can satisty competing or **conflicting interests**. A hypothetical ___ but highly unlikely ___ example of such an "open" system follows:

In the City of Delight, the incidence of residential burglary over the past year had increased 200 percent. The *police department* (a public organization responsible for management of certain public safety system) instituted a "system" for reducing the number of burglaries. This was called the Burglary Abatement Detail (BAD). A specially selected group of police officers were assigned to interrogate all "suspicious-looking" citizens in the residential to areas with the highest burglary rates. The "system results" were: (1) greatly reduced number of burglaries and (2) greatly increased number of **citizen complaints** of police harassment. Several system "corrections" were called for by citizens' groups. One correction was the issuance of citizens' identity cards, which , when visibly displayed on the person, reduced the chance of unnecessary interrogation

In this example, the system results were not accurately predicted, and given the results, **corrective decisions** were made outside the BAD system ___ an "open" system.

Public management systems are "open" for one or more of the following reasons:

1. System objectives often are not clear or are not complete .This means that system results can be interpreted differently by affected groups of citizens.

2. Often it is difficult to agree on meaningful measures of system results

3. System corrections cannot usually be determined very much in advance.

Unfavorable results require **individual interpretation** outside the system and, often, a unique correction or set of corrections. If the system variables are complex and insufficient time and effort have been spent analyzing them and their ramifications, results are even more unpredictable.

Helpful vocabulary:

open systems	أنظمة مفتوحة
interest groups	جماعات ذات مصالح، جماعات مصلحية
competing interests	مصالح متنافسة
hypothetical example	مثال افتراضي
residential burglary	السطو على المنازل
police department	دائرة الشرطة
to institute a system	يؤسس نظاماً
to interrogate	يستجوب
residential areas	مناطق سكنية
suspicious-looking citizens	مواطنون مريبو المظهر
police harassment	تحرُّش الشرطة
identity card	بطاقة الهوية
corrective decisions	قرارات تصحيحية
system objectives	أهداف النظام
meaningful measures	مقاييس ذات معنى
in advance	مُقَدَّماً، سَلَفاً
system variables	متغيرَّات النظام
individual interpretation	تفسير فردي
systems analysis	تحليل النظم
optimum public system	لنظام العام الأمثل
absolutely minimal	في حده الأدنى
regarding	فيما يتعلق بِ
public needs	الحاجات العامة
needs-assessment process	عملية تقييم الحاجات
conflicting interests	مصالح متصارعة

Exercise 1. Translate the previous passage into Arabic.

Exercise 2. *Fill in this table with the suitable English derivatives whenever possible, and write down the Arabic equivalents of all the words.*

Verb		Noun		Adjective	
English	**Arabic**	**English**	**Arabic**	**English**	**Arabic**
distinguish					
				public	
serve					
				open	
interact					
				residential	
satisfy					
		number			
				certain	
				suspicious	
reduce					
		result			
				corrective	
display					
		reason			
				entire	
complain					
		conclusion			

Exercise 3. *Translate these terms:*

police	————	————	result	————	————
call	————	————	issue	————	————
reason	————	————	time	————	————
display	————	————	complex	————	————
number	————	————	open	————	————

UNIT 6

PUBLIC AND PRIVATE SECTORS

The expression "*public sector*" and "*private sector*" are now very commonplace. The first refers to a system of organizations concerned with achieving State purposes. Public sector organizations include Government Departments, local authorities, and nationalized industries, all the subjects of later chapters. There is tremendous variety within this sector. The term "private sector", on the other hand, is used as a collective phrase referring to organisations which are neither State-owned, nor operating specifically to achieve State goals.

A popular view of the privet organisation is that built on the enterprise of an individual or a family, the typical example of such an organization being the business firm. Another linked view of such organizations is that they are headed by an entrepreneur, and ownership and control of the business are in his hands. Such a view of the business firm is much loved by *classical economists*, and whole industries are sometimes portrayed as being organized in this way. Competition takes place between the firms, and as result everybody benefits. Efficiency is rewarded and inefficiency is punished. Such a view of private business organizations is no longer appropriate; the day of the individual entrepreneur, with notable exceptions, is over. However, this model is a useful means of illustrating the widely reported differences between the public and the private sectors.

The first test of this difference is known as the **cui bono** test. This asks the question: who benefits from the organization? Or, put another way, whose goals does the organisation serve? The main beneficiary of the firm which is headed by a single individual and financed by his money is the **owner / manager**. The owner usually invests time and effort in establishing a business in the hope of making a profit. Profit is seen as the main motivating force of *a private enterprise economy*. The administration of such a firm is concerned with the management of men, materials, and the like, in such a way as to make it possible and practical to make a profit. Administration here is also concerned with the problem of "efficiency".

When the cui bono test is applied to the State organisations of the public sector, different results are obtained. For instance, it is difficult to recognize who the prime beneficiaries of many public sector organizations are. Is the *prime beneficiary* of the Department of Social Security the Minister in charge of it? Is it an individual applicant for welfare benefit at counter of **a local branch** of the Department?

Helpful vocabulary:

public sector	قطاع عام
private sector	قطاع خاص
state purpose	أهداف الدولة
government departments	دوائر حكومية
local authorities	سلطات محلية
nationalized industries	صناعات مؤممة
collective phrase	عبارة جامعة
state-owned	مملوكة من الدولة
classical economists	اقتصاديون تقليديون
is over	انتهى
put another way	بعبارة أخرى
main beneficiary	المستفيد الرئيسي
owner/ manager	المدير المالك
motivating force	القوة الدافعة
public interest	المصلحة العامة
commitment to	التزام بـ
Ministry of Defence	وزارة الدفاع
nuclear defence capability	قدرة دفاعية نووية
state pensions	رواتب الدولة التقاعدية
individual entrepreneur	مالك فردي
to assess profitablility	يقيِّم الرِّبحية
nuclear submarine	غواصة نووية
to take into account	يأخذ في الاعتبار
unprofitable service	خدمات غير ربحية
housing policy	سياسة إسكانية

38

Exercise 1. *Translate the previous passage into Arabic*

Exercise 2. *Fill in this table with the suitable English derivatives whenever possible, and write down the Arabic equivalents of all the words.*

Verb		Noun		Adjective	
English	**Arabic**	**English**	**Arabic**	**English**	**Arabic**
refer					
				private	
achieve					
vary					
		economist			
collect					
		model			
operate				nuclear	
link					
		beneficiary			
report					
				local	
		profit	·		
manage					
				complete	
		industry			
finance					
				efficient	
serve					

Exercise 3. *Translate these terms:*

accrued assets	_____	accrued interest	_____
accrued dividend	_____	accrued leave	_____
accrued expenses	_____	debt acknowledgement	_____
accrued income	_____	actionable negligence	_____
time of delivery	_____	time draft	_____

UNIT 7

APPROACHES TO MANAGEMENT
AND ADMINISTRAITON
DEVELOPMENT

The problems of administration and management in
developing economies arise from a rapid change in expectations
which is not matched by appropriate organizational and
institutional change .gaps are seen in the capability and efficiency of
established institutions to attain social goals, and gaps are seen in
established structures, systems, and functions appropriate for new
human values and relationships. These gap cannot be adequately
filled by international transfers of resources, nor can they be
completely removed by vast new educational efforts Institution and
system building for the public and private sectors of the developing
economy, while an intrinsic aspect of the development process,
contribute only a fraction of the inputs of the complex process.

In this chapter, the author seeks to survey the issues of
management and administration related to organizational change
and system building in **economic development**. He does not
propose or expect to touch on all the problems or to assign orders
of importance to issues identified, let alone suggest universally
satisfying solutions to the difficulties of the " Soft State" .

To a large degree, the terms "management" and "administration" are used in this paper interchangeably. This reflects a growing tendency in the literature and in practice, especially in dealing with economic development to view the management and administration of the economy and change as much the same operation. Management thinking in government is increasing in both developed and developing countries. National planning and **policy development** are forced on administrative groups in developing economies, and even managers of *non-government organizations* are forced to work within the guidelines of carefully defined national goals. Thus, administrators adopt managerial roles, and managers become administrators in seeking to achieve development objectives.

This convergence of roles occurs despite a continuing sense of administration as an ongoing subservient role and management as a shorter-term *controlling role*. Administration is usually thought of as accepting goals from outside the system, as depending upon resources from other systems, and as being instructed in the use if means. Management, on the other hand, is usually thought of as developing goal within the system, using resources over which the system has control, and being free in the use of means. Receiving its authority from outside (or above) and referring its decisions and results elsewhere, administration involves an **instrumental relationship**, whereas the manager is self – contained and acts as principal rather than as agent.

Helpful Vocabulary:

administrative development	تنمية إدارية
developing economies	اقتصاديات نامية
transfer of resources	انتقال الموارد
intrinsic aspect	مظهر داخلي
development processes	عملية تنمية
system building	بناء النظام
let alone	ناهيكَ عَنْ
national planning	تخطيط قومي
policy development	تطوير السياسات
developed countries	بلدان متقدمة
developing countries	بلدان نامية
convergence of roles	تلاقي الأدوار، اختلاط الأدوار
management thinking	تفكير إداري
instrumental relationship	علامة نفعية
administrative important	تحسين إداري
individual recipient	مستقبل فردي
agencies of government	وكالات حكومية
multinational corporation	شركة متعددة الجنسيات
individual finances	تمويلات فردية
national development	تنمية قومية، تنمية وطنية
computer technology	تِقَانَةُ الحاسوب، تِقْنية الحاسوب
operations research	بحوث العمليات
system analysis	تحليل النظم
cost-benefit analysis	تحليل التكاليف والعائدات
knowledge utilization	الانتفاع بالمعرفة

Exercise 1. Translate the previous passage into Arabic

Exercise 2. *Fill in this table with the suitable English derivatives whenever possible, and write down the Arabic equivalents of all the words.*

Verb		Noun		Adjective	
English	**Arabic**	**English**	**Arabic**	**English**	**Arabic**
develop					
		change			
attain					
		institution			
establish					
		value			
transfer					
		solution			
contribute					
		operation			
Build					
touch					
		progress			
reflect					
		mechanics			
define					

Exercise 3. *Translate these terms:*

active account	———————	active stock	———————
active asset	———————	active trade balance	———————
active capital	———————	actual asset	———————
active market	———————	tied loan	———————
active partner		tied shop	

UNIT 8

THE DEMANDS OF INDEPENDCE
UPON PUBLIC *ADMINISTRATION*

The term "development administration " came into use in the 1950s to represent those aspects of public administration and those changes in public administration which are needed to carry out policies, projects, and programs to improve social and economic conditions. During a period of fifteen years following the end of World War II, in 1945, colony after colony threw off the imperial yoke. Country after country achieved independence and **political autonomy** .this new status gave promise of freedom and liberty and self-determination in political systems of representative democracy .It gave hope of greater individual freedom equality of treatment in the society. And independence created hops of higher national and per capita income, a rapid rise in standards of living and an increase in individual opportunity.

Even in countries which had not been colonies but had been administered by some other from of *authoritarian government*, this was a generation of rising and insistent expectations pressing for rapid political, social, and economic change. New governments and their bureaucracies their administrative agencies and processes, were expected to give reality to these anticipated fruits of independence and liberty. These new functions, these demands upon the administration system, were not only enormous in size and weight, they were novel and complex in character.

An urgent and perhaps the first task of anew country was to establish its identity as a unified and integrated nation-state and to create a new system for deciding policy and for making decisions. This political development involved building a valid and recognized hegemony internally and achieving recognition externally by establishing effective communications and relationships with other countries and the **international community**. The task of building a national polity required the accommodation of diverse and even disparate social, tribal, and ethnic groups in the population. A foreign policy to achieve *international recognition* and amity involved the creation of a foreign service. At the same time, numerous and demanding specific needs had to be met by each new country at independence and by its new, inexperienced government and ill-equipped bureaucracy. Taxes had to be assessed and arrangements made for their collection. Courts and continuity of justice had to be assured.

Perhaps even more important and more difficult than establishing its identity was the task of a new country to diverse a system to translate the *aspirations and demands* of its population into viable policies and programs, a responsive process for making decisions on major matters.

Helpful vocabulary:

development administration	إدارة التنمية
policies , projects, and programs	سياسات ومشاريع وبرامج
economic conditions	ظروف اقتصادية
imperial yoke	نِير الاستعمار
colony after colony	مُسْتَعْمرةٌ تِلْوَ مستعمرةٍ
political autonomy	استقلال سياسي
to give promise of	يُبَشِّر بِ
per capita income	دخل الفرد
standards of living	مستويات المعيشة
authoritarian government	حكومة متسلطة
anticipated fruits	ثمار متوقعة
demands upon	متطلبات من
novel and complex	جديدة ومعقدة
deciding policy	تقرير السياسة
to achieve recognition	يحصل على الاعتراف
international community	المجتمع الدولي
international recognition	اعتراف دولي
demanding needs	حاجات مُلِحَّة
to be met	تُسْتَوْفى
aspirations and demands	الطموحات والمطالب
representative democracy	ديمقراطية تمثيلية
some system of	نظام من نوع ما
elected executive	هيئات تنفيذية منتخبة
correction of injustices	تصحيح المظالم، رفع المظالم
land tenure systems	أنظمة امتلاك الأراضي

Exercise 1. *Translate the previous passage into Arabic*

Exercise 2. *Fill in this table with the suitable English derivatives whenever possible, and write down the Arabic equivalents of all the words*

Verb		Noun		Adjective	
English	Arabic	English	Arabic	English	Arabic
		Public			
		program			
Improve					
		period			
		independence			
		Equality			
				national	
				Individual	
		freedom			
				insistent	
		fruit			
				novel	
demand					
		Election			
				complex	
decide					
involve					
		aspiration			

Exercise 3. *Translate these terms:*

actual cost	_____	actual total loss	_____
actual delivery	_____	added value	_____
actual loss	_____	trade association	_____
actual partner	_____	trade balance	_____

47

UNIT 9

THE USEFULNESS OF STATISTICS TO PUBLIC ADMINISTRATION

Whether in universities, police departments, or health agencies, bureaucracies increasingly rely on statistics and quantitative measures for information about the scope and success of their programs. University administrators calculate enrollment and credit-hour statistics to justify moving funds from departments of philosophy to those of engineering; police administrators gather and process crime data to convince the public that the police department needs a larger budget; health planning administrators use **statistic** to justify their decision that no new hospitals should be built in a community. Both administrators and social scientists have used statistics to persuade federal courts that policies relating to such issues as school finance, integration, affirmative action, jury selection, and so forth are unconstitutional. In each of these cases, policy decisions are based at least in part on the results quantitative analyses.

Furthermore, low- and middle-level bureaucrats are constantly pressed to collect, maintain, and present data to show their departments'

Productivity and problems. How many miles of highway were built in 1987? How many mental health clients were treated last year? How many participants in alternative sentencing programs committed another crime? How many applicants for drivers' licenses had to wait more than one hour? *Descriptive measures* such as these are crucial to agencies in justifying their existence and budget to taxpayers, policymakers, and clients.

The following are specific examples illustrating some common situations where **quantitative methods** are crucial.

1. A local United Way agency wants to find out if its distribution of United Way funds meets with community approval, if there are unmet needs which the community favors meeting, and if the United Way appeal is efficiently reaching likely donors. To answer these questions, someone in the agency must be aware of the appropriate quantitative methods. Agency personnel who would likely contract out this project to a survey research firm must be sophisticated enough in quantitative methodology to be able to frame the questions they want answered and to evaluate critically the data collection procedures and results presented to them by the survey research consulting firm.

2. A state converts to a zero-based **budgeting system** Agency and department heads are called upon to collect, maintain, and present data on an annual basis which will allow each portion of each state agency to be evaluated on its cost per unit service delivered.

Helpful vocabulary:

police departments	دوائر الشرطة
quantitative measures	مقاييس كمية
university administrators	إداريو الجامعة
credit- hour statistics	إحصائيات الساعات المعتمدة
moving funds	نقل الأرصدة
crime data	بيانات عن الجرائم
school finance	تمويل المدارس
jury selection	اختيار المحلَّفين
at least in part	على الأقل جزئياً
quantitative analyses	تحليلات كمية
mental health clients	مراجعو الصحة النفسية
alternative sentencing programs	برامج الأحكام البديلة
drivers' licenses	إجازات السياقة
descriptive measures	مقاييس وصفية
unmet needs	حاجات غير مستوفاة
likely donors	متبرعون محتملون
to be aware of	أن يكون عارفاً بـ
data collection procedures	إجراءات جمع البيانات
survey research consulting firm	شركة استشارية للبحوث المسحية
department heads	رؤساء الدوائر
state agency	وكالة رسمية
to evaluate on	يقيِّم على أساس
cost per unit	كلفة الوحدة
uniformed officers	ضباط في الخدمة
downtown area	منطقة وسط المدينة

Exercise 1. *Translate the previous passage into Arabic*

Exercise 2. *Fill in this table with the suitable English derivatives whenever possible, and write down the Arabic equivalents of all the words*

Verb		Noun		Adjective	
English	**Arabic**	**English**	**Arabic**	**English**	**Arabic**
		health			
increase					
rely					
		quantity			
				social	
		equality			
measure					
justify					
		process			
				alternative	
move					
gather					
		hospital			
base					
		school			
affirm					
		statistics			
integrate					
		existence			
treat					
		participant			

Exercise 3. *Translate these terms:*

administrative advisor	_____	administrative functions	_____
administrative affairs	_____	administrative head	_____
administrative assistant	_____	administrative officer	_____
administrative authority	_____	administrative policy	_____
administrative expenses	_____	administrative reform	_____

51

UNIT 10

IMAGS OF PUBLIC ADMINISTRAITON

Similarly, we cannot speak of public administration without having in mind certain models or *a priori* conceptions of how an administrative system works, just as we have ideas about how a market system works - how prices are adjusted to equalize supply and demand. In the case of administration, this basic model assumes the existence of a structurally distinct government subject to control by a political organization, such as political parties, parliament, public opinion, popular suffrage, and interest groups. This political organization, established according to a formula called the "constitution" lays down a set of goals and policies known as "laws" and "regulations".

Under the control of this organization, there is an *administrative apparatus* or bureaucracy charged with the task of implementing the laws. The bureaucracy is supposed to be politically "neutral"; it does not participate in **policy determination**, it has no specific interests of its obedient servant of the government, hence, of the public whom the regime serves.

The chief questions in public administration arise under this set of assumptions. If the laws are to be carried out if , at the same time ,the resources in *public funds*, skilled personnel , buildings ,and equipment are limited , then what is the most "efficient" way in which these scarce means can be mobilized to achieve the desired goals to the maximum extent ?

When phrased this way, it will be seen that the basic model of public administration is analogous to the *market model*. In both instances, the resources to be dispread are considered as scarce , the goals to be accomplished as given — to maximize profits, to implement polices — and hence the objective to be the "rational" allocation of human and material means. Both administration and economics, in other words, assume a situation in which choices can and must be made because if insufficient means.

Karl Polanyi, in the book referred to above , distinguishes between *formal economics*, which deals with the assumed market model just described, and *substantive economics*, which deals with the ways in which humans beings interact with their natural and **social environments** so as to satisfy their material wants. From this viewpoin, substantive economics may include situations of insufficiency in which nevertheless no choices are made, or choices are made where no insufficiency exists.

Helpful vocabulary:

to have in mind	يتذكر
a period conception	مفاهيم مسبقة
market system	نظام السُّوق
supply and demand	العَرض والطلب
subject to control	خاضعة للسيطرة
public option	الرأي العام
according to a formula	طبقاً لصيغة
administrative apparatus	جهاز إداري
charged with	مسؤولة عن
politically neutral	محايد سياسياً
interests of its own	مصالح خاصة بها
obedient servant	خادم مطيع
hence	من ثَمَّ
set of assumptions	مجموعة افتراضات
public funds	الأموال العامة
to maximize profits	إلى الحد العامة
market or exchange	سوق التبادلات
situation of insufficiency	مواقف عدم الكفاية
administrative behavior	سلوك إداري
let us assume	دعنا نفترض
set forth above	المبيَّة أعلاه
a set of office	مجموعة من الموظفين
to a sense	يشعر أنّ
at work	يعمل

Exercise 1. *Translate the previous passage into Arabic*

Exercise 2. *Fill in this table with the suitable English derivatives whenever possible, and write down the Arabic equivalents of all the words*

Verb		Noun		Adjective	
English	**Arabic**	**English**	**Arabic**	**English**	**Arabic**
		conception			
work					
				basic	
adjust					
		Demand			
Equalize					
				distinct	
assume					
		Constitution			
				popular	
exist					
charge					
		regulation			
				obedient	
suppose					
		Interest			
				maximal	
		Exercise			
				scarce	
implement					
		allocation			

Exercise 3. *Translate these terms:*

advertising allowance	_____	advertising medium	_____
advertising appropriation	_____	advisory board	_____
advertising campaign	_____	advisory body	_____
advertising costs	_____	trade fair	_____
advertising directory	_____	trade directory	_____

UNIT 11

MANAGEMENT
MADE SIMPLE

It is important, with the space-age future in mind, to assess the main factors which motivate Britain's manager today. At first sight, it might appear that high salaries would be the main attraction, but financial incentives in business have their limits net of tax. *Fringe benefits* (special pension schemes, company cars, executive dining- rooms, foreign travel, expense accounts, etc.) are also subject to fiscal control.

Nevertheless, with promotion through the hierarchy, it is still possible to achieve an increasing standard of living, subject, of course, to inflation and *government incomes policies*. Once certain acceptable standards have been achieved, however, every effort will usually be made to keep them.

Disincentives .Yet ,in any questionnaire completed by top or other levels of management on the subject of motivation, financial incentives tend to be well down the list in order of importance. At any point, too, managers could well be expected to stop and weigh up the time, effort, and risk involved in taking on more arduous responsibilities, against the satisfactions that they and their families would be likely to gain from extra pay .promotions within the firm, or by joining another firm, usually cause domestic disturbance, perhaps more travel , and increased expenses, to say nothing of additional worry. Money alone then seems hardly the best way to stimulate *managerial performance* or motivate mobility.

Non-Financial Aspects. The answer can usually be found in *noun-financial incentives*. Top rating in questionnaire assessments is often given to personal achievements, measured against mutually acceptable company targets, and the recognition given to those achievements. Then there is the interest of the job itself, the satisfaction derived from doing it well, and of sharing in the firm's successes – usually measured by rate of growth and increased profitability. Allied factors usually mentioned are promotion prospects, opportunities for taking on increased responsibilities, the nature of the work itself, job security, and the climate of work. In the successful firm, there is usually managerial drive, excitement, a sense of urgency, and a feeling of power. Yet, fortunately, few managers seek such power merely for the sake of power.

Public recognition, too, attaches to the top jobs, and *social satisfactions* can often be felt through the impact on the man in the street of decisions made concerning goods or services offered.

Helpful vocabulary:

At first sight	لأول نظرة، بالنظرة الأولى
Financial Incentives	الحوافز المالية
Fringe benefits	فوائد إضافية
standard of living	مستوى معيشة
subject of inflation	مُعَّرض للتضخم
Subject of motivation	موضوع الدافعية
extra pay	المدفوعات الإضافية
managerial performance	الأداء الإداري
non – financial incentive	حوافز غير مالية
measured against	مقاسة حَسْبَ
rate of growth	معدل النمو
promotion prospects	فُرَصُ الترقية
job security	الأمن الوظيفي
recognition of achievement	الاعتراف بالإنجاز، تقدير الإنجاز
at a time of no growth	في وقت لا نموَّ فيه
inspired resignation	استقالة موحى بها
straight dismissal	إقالة مباشرة
costly passengers	المسافرون المُكَلِّفون
pyramid of promotion	هَرَمُ الترقية
clear line of command	خط قيادي واضح
trainee managers	مدراء متدربون
school of experience	مدرسة الخبرة
higher degree	درجة عليا
experienced seniors	رؤساء ذوو خبرة
managerial generation gap	الفجوة الإدارية بين الأجياب

Exercise 1. *Translate the previous passage into Arabic*

Exercise 2. *Fill in this table with the suitable English derivatives whenever possible, and write down the Arabic equivalents of all the words*

Verb		Noun		Adjective	
English	Arabic	English	Arabic	English	Arabic
assess					
concentrate					
		factor			
recognize					
		power			
increase					
		growth			
				Inspired	
add					
		resignation			
				clear	
weigh					
		dismissal			
				Wise	
		worry			
				experienced	
disturb					

Exercise 3. *Translate these terms:*

affiliated company   ——————   agreed charges   ——————

aged poor   ——————   agreed price   ——————

agent   ——————   air transport   ——————

air mail   ——————   age of discretion   ——————

aggregate demand   ——————   airway bill   ——————

UNIT 12

ADMINISTRATIVE LAW

It is a commonplace among administrative lawyers that Dicey is responsible for the subject having a "bad name" in this country. This is indeed a fact brought home to most constitutional law students early in their legal career after tackling the rule of law. Dicey's dislike of administrative law is, of course, readily apparent from the *Law of the Constitution*. We have, however, to push further if we are to understand in more detail how Dicey's views have coloured administrative law. What did this scholar actually do which was to have such a lasting effect on our subject? What Dicey actually did was to base his view of administrative law on a certain view of democracy which can be termed **unitary**. This is not a difficult idea and may be explained as follows.

First, all students are aware of the sovereignty of parliament in the sense that parliament is Omnicompetent. It can ban smoking in Pairs or repeal the grant of independence to former colonies. Less well known is an equally important aspect of sovereignty which may be termed *parliamentary monopoly*. This means that all governmental power should be channeled through parliament in order that it might be subject to legitimation and oversight by the Commons. There was a belief in the nineteenth century, albeit not universally shared but held by Dicey, that the Commons could and did control the **executive**, and that all public power should be subject to legislative oversight.

Second, dicey then used the rule of law to reinforce sovereignty in the sense of parliamentary nonopoly. How did he achieve this? The Diceyan role of law has what may be termed both a descriptive and a normative content. In *descriptive terms*, it was assumed that the regular law predominated, that exercise of broad discretionary power was absent, and that all people were subject to the ordinary law of the realm .All public power did in fact reside with parliament .In *normative terms*, it was assumed that this was indeed a better system than that which existed in France, where special rules and a distinctive regime existed for public law matters. It was "good" that all law should be regular law, duly enacted and legitimated by parliament.

Thus democracy was, for Dicey, unitary in the sense that all public power was channelled through parliament. This democratic system was also "self-correcting" in that Dicey believed that the Commons accurately reflected the *will of the people* and controlled the executive. The all-powerful parliament would not, therefore, be likely to pass legislation which was contrary to the wishes of the electorate.

Helpful vocabulary:

having a bad name	سيء الصيِّت
a fact brought home to	حقيقة يعرفها
the rule of law	حكم القانون
administrative law	القانون الإداري
lasting effect	تأثير دائم
unitary democracy	ديمقراطية أحادية
aspect of sovereignty	أحد مظاهر السيادة
parliamentary monopoly	احتكار برلماني
subject to legitimation	خاضع للتشريع
public power	سلطة الجمهور
to reside with	تقع في يد
in descriptive terms	بنظرة وصفية
in descriptive	بنظرة معيارية
in the sense that	بمعنى أن
the wishes of the electorate	رغبات الناخبين
executive attention	اهتمام واسع
notwithstanding this error	بالرغم من الخطأ
fitting base	قاعدة ملائمة
unfit for habitation	غير صالح للسكن
judicial intervention	تدخل قضائي
sovereign will	الإرادة السيادية
real legislature	المشرِّع الحقيقي
to police bound	يراقب الحدود
in striving to attain	في الكفاح لتحقيق
illegally treated	عوامل بطريقة غير قانونية

Exercise 1. *Translate the previous passage into Arabic*

Exercise 2. *Fill in this table with the suitable English derivatives whenever possible, and write down the Arabic equivalents of all the words*

Present		Past	Past Participle	Present participle
English	Arabic			
is				
bring				
tackle				
have				
push				
push				
understand				
color				
do				
last				
ban				
know				
channel				
share				
reinforce				
hold				
assume				
exist				
provide				

Exercise 3. *Translate these terms*:

allotment of shares	_____	amortized loan	_____
allowance system	_____	annual budge	_____
all- risks policy	_____	annual increment	_____
all risks insurance	_____	annual increment	_____
amicable settlement	_____	annual return	_____

UNIT 13

FACTORS INFLUENCING
PRODUCTIVITY

Four major factors have contributed to the declining growth rate in productivity: (1) declining capital intensity, (2) declining expenditures on research and development, (3) changes in the composition of the labor force and the economy, and (4) changing societal attitudes and values. These factors are considered in turn.

Declining Capital Intensity

One way to measure *capital intensity* is in terms of capital outlays per worker. From 1950 to 1972, the average annual growth rate in capital outlays per worker was 2.9 percent; however, from 1972 to 1979, the average annual growth rate was 0.6 percent. Had the prior growth rate been maintained, the capital stock in 1979 would have been $200 bullion larger. A second measure of capital intensity is in terms of **gross national product (GNP)**. In 1980, expenditures on capital were approximately 10 percent of GNP compared to roughly 20 percent in Japan. At least six factors have contributed to the Decline in capital intensity.

Tax policies. In 1969, capital gains taxes were nearly doubled and they were raised again in 1976 to almost 50 percent. Consequently, if an asset appreciated by 40 percent, and one-half the increase were due to inflation, the *capital gains tax* equaled the entire noinflationary gain. Not surprisingly, between 1969 and 1978 (when capital gains taxes were lowered), some 6 million investors dropped out of the capital markets, and new venture financing virtually disappears. The capital gains tax has since been reduced again, resulting (apparently) in the dramatic increase in capital commitments shown in Figure1-3.

Inflation. One impact of the inflationary environment of the 1970s was an increase in *personal tax rates* via "bracket creep"; concomitantly there was a decrease in personal savings. Inflation did not merely reduce savings, it also affected investment choices: large sums were invested in passive hedges against inflation such as collectibles, e.g., precious metals, oriental rugs, stamps, vintage wines, and various other nonproductive assets. Further, inflation caused corporate earnings to be overstated to the extent that inventory and depreciation expenses were less than current replacement costs. Capital investment, in effect, was taxed by inflation

Growth in the Public Sector. Evidence accumulated by the Hudson Institute in Europe indicates that the larger an economy's public sector, the slower the rate of *economic growth* (see Figure 1-4).

Helpful Vocabulary:

declining growth rate	المعدل المتناقص للنمو ، معدل النمو المتناقص
expenditures on research	النفقات على البحث
composition of the labor force	تكوين قوة العمل
changing social attitudes	المواقف المجتمعية المتغيرة
per worker	لكل عاملٍ
average annual growth rate	متوسط نسبة النمو السنوي
had it been maintained	لو حوفظ عليها
gross national product(GNP)	الناتج القومي الإجمالي
due to out of	السياسات الضريبية
tax policies	بسبب التضخم
to drop out of	ينسحب من
capital marker	أسواق رأس المال
resulting in	مؤدية إلى
inflationary environment	بيئة التضخّم
personal tax rate	معدل الضريبة الشخصية
depreciation expenses	تكاليف هبوط القيمة
in effect	نتيجة لذلك
public sector	القطاع العام
the larger , the slower	كلما كان أكبر ، كان ابطأ
to account for	يفسر
shrinking profits	أرباح متناقصة
energy costs	تكاليف الطاقة
not mere coincidence	لَيس مجرد صدفة
sharp slowdown	التباطؤ حاد
energy crisis	أزمة الطاقة

Exercise 1. *Translate the previous passage into Arabic*

Exercise 2. *Fill in this table with the suitable English derivatives whenever possible, and write down the Arabic equivalents of all the words*

Verb		Noun		Adjective	
English	**Arabic**	**English**	**Arabic**	**English**	**Arabic**
decline					
		productivity			
measure					
		intensity			
				national	
		research			
work					
		change			
				Intense	
		value			
contribute					
		average			
				slow	
grow					
		orient			
				evident	
reduce					
commit					

Exercise 3. *Translate these terms*:

anti-menology	_____	applied economics	_____
anti-inflation	_____	appointee	_____
quotation	_____	aptitude test	_____
applied accounting	_____	arbitration	_____

UNIT 14

FINANCIAL MANAGEMENT

The complexity of American hospitals and *health care organization* has grown dramatically, especially in the past ten years. It is commonly recognized that some hospitals in America will be forced to close as this growth in administrative, as well as financial, complexity continues .The chief financial officer will play one of the most important roles in the game of survival. In this chapter, we will see how this position has evolved.

THE EVOLUTION OF FINANCIAL MANAGEMEN

Health car finance has evolved from a primitive function of bookkeeping / accounting to a role in which it exerts a major influence on the management of *health care organizations*, the allocation of scarce resources, and strategic planning. To help us understand this change, let us look at how the function of hospital financial management has evolved.

Before Government Involvement

Before Medicare, Medicaid, and other widespread government programs, the typical American hospital needed little more than simple bookkeeping. Once a year a decision was made to raise prices.The decision process was not very complex, and a good administrator could easily calculate the needed price increases in less than a day. There was no need for a **detailed budget,** no need for a cost accounting system, and no cost reports to be filed. Hospitals had the very successful, and philanthropy was common. If money persisted as a problem, the hospital simply raised prices again.

Through the middle 1960s, the top financial position was often *chief accountant* or supervisor of accounting. This was sometimes filed by a dependable employee with a high school education and many years of seniority. The supervisor of accounting reported to an assistant administrator, and from 10 to 15 other departments also reported to this position. Accounting was that necessary evil; it did not contribute directly to the hospital's mission in the minds of many administrators or in the minds of many board members.

The Influence of Government

In 1966 we saw the first Medicare cost reports. These cost reports assumes a *cost accounting system* that hospitals did not have the expertise to develop. This was followed by Medicaid cost reports. In those early years, the assistant administrator struggled through the cost reports with the chief accountant, or the job was given to independent outside auditors. Neither did a very good job by today's standards, but then the intermediaries were not very astute , so it did not make very much difference .

Helpful vocabulary:

financial management	الإدارة المالية
health care organizations	منظمة الرعاية الصحية
commonly recognized	معترفٌ به على نحو شائع
game of survival	لعبة البقاء
allocation of resources	تخصيص الموارد
widespread government programs	برامج حكومية واسعة الانتشار
price increases	زيادات الأسعار
decision process	عملية اتخاذ القرار
detailed budget	موازنة مفصّلة
cost accounting system	نظام محاسبة التكاليف
chief accountant	المحاسب الرئيسي، رئيس المحاسبين
supervisor of accounting	مشرف محاسبي
dependable employee	موظف موثوق به
years of seniority	سنوات من الأقدمية
necessary evil	شَرٌّ لا بد منه
independent outside auditor	مدقق خارجي مستقل
today's standards	معايير اليوم
assistant administrator	الإداري المساعد
accounting information needs	الحاجات إلى المعلومات المحاسبية
economic Stabilization Act	قانون الاستقرار الاقتصادي، مرسوم الاستقرار الاقتصادي
ran out of cash	لم يبق لديها سيولة نقدية
maybe	من المحتمل
to control inflation	يسيطر على التضخم
political arena	الحلبة السياسية
person's life saving	مدخرات الشخص طيلة حياته

Exercise 1. *Translate the previous passage into Arabic*

Exercise 2. *Fill in this table with the suitable English derivatives whenever possible, and write down the Arabic equivalents of all the words*

Verb		Noun		Adjective	
English	Arabic	English	Arabic	English	Arabic
		health			
				complex	
force					
		hospital			
		Position			
close				Primitive	
evolve				simple	
raise		function			
cost		plan			
		philanthropy			
				imaginative	
file					

Exercise 3. Translate these terms:

arbitration	_____	assets	_____
as per advice	_____	liabilities	_____
as per instructions	_____	assistant manager	_____
as per contract	_____	assistant secretary	_____
assembly line	_____	trade disputes	_____

UNIT 15

THREE FINANCIAL TARGETS

We now confine our attention to a New Keynesian strategy. In this case, employment is to be promoted by the fixing of wage rates at appropriate levels. This has been discussed at length in volume 1, and no purpose would be served by repeating that discussion here. This wage-fixing is to be carried out against a background of demand- management policies designed to keep the **total money expenditure** on goods and services produced in the **UK**, and so the total money income earned in their production, on a steady growth path. This path for domestically produced money incomes we will call the money income target.

UP to this point, we have discussed this target as if it were the only target with which we need be concerned in devising a set of financial controls through fiscal, monetary, and **foreign-exchange policies**. But in fact it is not possible to overlook the effect of such a set of financial controls on the balance of payments and on the distribution of the national product between current consumption and capital development for future use. We must in fact think of a set of the retargets –the total of domestically produced money incomes, the balance of payments with the rest of the world, and the ratio of capital investment to *current consumption* ‒ as being controlled by three sets of financial instruments ‒ fiscal policy, monetary policy, and exchange-rate policy.

Accordingly, in this chapter we discuss the nature of the three *financial targets*, in chapter IV we discuss the nature of the three weapons of financial control, and in chapter V the way in which the use of the weapons might best be designed for the successful achievement of the three financial targets.

The Money Income Target: Coverage

We start with a discussion of the choice of the most appropriate money income target to represent the total of *money incomes* generated by the production of goods and services in the UK. Table III.1 illustrates the nature of the choice.

Items 1, 2 and 3 of the table together constitute the 'net domestic product at factor cost' (item 4). This represents the sum of the earned and unearned incomes (wages, salaries, profits, and rents) received from employment in the UK of real resources of labor, *capital goods* , land ,and natural resources for the production of goods and services for sale for final use (1) by the government, (2) by persons or businesses in the UK for consumption or to add to their capital equipment, or (3) by foreigners.

Helpful Vocabulary:

to confine our attention	لحصر اهتمامنا
financial targets	أهداف مالية
money income	الدخل النقدي
balance of payments	ميزان المدفوعات
investment ratio	نسبة إستثمار
fixing of wage rates	الأجور تثبيت معدلات
at length	بالتفصيل
total money expenditure	الإنفاق النقدي الكلي
domestically produced money incomes	مداخيل نقدية محليا
fiscal policy	سياسة مالية
monetary policy	سياسة نقدية
foreign – exchange policy	سياسة صرف العملات الأجنبية
current consumption	الاستهلاك الحالي
capital development	تنمية رأس المال
financial control	الرقابة المالية
good and services	السِّلع والخدمات
net profits	الأرباح الصافية ، صافي الأرباح
gross domestic product	الناتج المحلي الإجمالي
net income	صافي الدخل
market prices	أسعار السوق
depiction in value	هبوط القيمة
capital goods	سلع رأسمالية
sales value	قيمة المبيعات
reduction in value	نقصان القيمة
deduction of the amount	حَسْم مبلغ

74

Exercise 1. *Translate the previous passage into Arabic.*

Exercise 2. *Fill in this table with the suitable English derivatives whenever possible, and write down the Arabic equivalents of all the words.*

Verb		Noun		Adjective	
English	Arabic	English	Arabic	English	Arabic
confine					
		attention			
promote					
				appropriate	
		level			
fix					
		purpose			
				Current	
design					
		target			
				Monetary	
devise					
		exchange			
				Profitable	
discuss					
		balance			
exist					
		Payment			
generate					
		table			

Exercise 3. Translate these terms:

attorney general	⎯⎯⎯⎯⎯	authorized capital	⎯⎯⎯⎯⎯
auction sale	⎯⎯⎯⎯⎯	authorized signature	⎯⎯⎯⎯⎯
audit bureau	⎯⎯⎯⎯⎯	authorized stock	⎯⎯⎯⎯⎯
auditor	⎯⎯⎯⎯⎯	auto-financing	⎯⎯⎯⎯⎯
auditing	⎯⎯⎯⎯⎯	automatic saving	⎯⎯⎯⎯⎯

UNIT 16

OPERATING ENVIRONMENT OF FINANCIAL MANAGEMENT

In making financial decisions which seek to increase the wealth of a firm's owner, a number of important external factors provide essential inputs into the *decision-making process*. These factors, or variables, are: (1) forms of business organizations, (2) the economic environment, (3) financial markets and intermediaries, and (4) corporate taxation.

This chapter stresses the importance of appreciating the impacts of the operating environment when dealing with specific functions of *financial management*. However, it is not possible to present all or even most of the details concerning the four variables of the operating environment mentioned above. Entire books have been written on each of these topics, so that an extended discussion is best left to more advanced and specialized financial management texts.

CHARATERISTICOFBUSINESSORGANIZATIONA FORMS

There were almost 14 million business firms operating in the United States during 1977. Sole proprietorships accounted for 78% of this total, provided 9% of total receipts, and earned 23% of total profits. While there were just over two million corporations doing business during the same **time span**, they produced 87% of total revenues and earned 73% of total profits. This very large percentage of total receipts and profits earned by corporations makes them the dominant organizational business from in this country. That is why this textbook concentrates on the financial management of corporations.

A sole proprietorship is simply a business owned by one person which has no legal standing apart from its owner. The owner, or proprietor, assumes all the risks of running the business. In particular, the proprietor is faced with unlimited liability. This means that business creditors can look to the owner's **personal assets** in order to satisfy business claims. In return for assuming these risks, the owner realizes all the profits and losses generated by the business. These profits and losses are taxed at *personal income tax rates.*

Financing the growth of the business is difficult because the proprietorship dose not issue debt or equity securities. The proprietor is responsible for meeting the terms of any **business loan** obtained, regardless of what happens to the business.

Transferring ownership of the proprietorship presents two problems. First, there is not transferable *evidence of ownership* even though certain licenses may be transferable. Second, measuring the value of the business in order to determine a selling price may be difficult.

Helpful vocabulary:

to seek to	يهدف إلى
firm's owners	مالكو الشركة
essential inputs	مُدخلات أساسية
decision-making process	عملية صُنْع القرار
corporate taxation	ضرائب الشركات
financial markets	الأسواق المالية
financial management	الإدارة المالية
operating environment	البيئة المؤثرة
sole proprietorship	مِلكية فردية
total profit	إجمالي الارباح
total receipts	إجمالي الإيصالات
time span	الفترة الزمنية
total revenues	إجمالي العوائد
management of corporation	إدارة الشركات
in particular	بوجه خاص ، على الأخص
profits and losses	الأرباح والخسائر
personal income tax	ضريبة الدخل الشخصية
business loan	قرض تجاري
to meet the terms	يفي بالشروط
current owner	المالك الحالي
prospective owner	المالك المتوقّع
transferring ownership	نقل الملكية
legal standing	الوضع القانوني
contractual obligations	التزامات تعاقدية
deceased partner	شريك مُتوفي

Exercise 1. *Translate the previous passage into Arabic.*

Exercise 2. *Fill in this table with the suitable English derivatives whenever possible, and write down the Arabic equivalents of all the words.*

Verb		Noun		Adjective	
English	Arabic	English	Arabic	English	Arabic
		wealth			
appreciate					
		number			
				financial	
		variable			
do					
		management			
				specialized	
		environment			
				advanced	
earn					
		profit			
				dominant	
own					
		loss			
				responsible	
measure					
		receipt			

Exercise 3. *Translate these terms*:

banking a bill	———————	bad check	———————
back label	———————	bad debt	———————
back pay	———————	bad deliver	———————
back order	———————	bail	———————
balance of trade	———————	bail bond	———————

UNIT 17

PRIVATE SECTOR AND PUBLIC SECTOR

Industrial development in India is of comparatively recent origin. During the British period, India had been looked upon as a source of raw-materials and market for finished goods only. Hence, the then Government never made any appreciable attempts for a *systematic development* of industries in spite of the fact that the raw-materials required for industries such as cotton, textiles, iron, steel, chemicals and pharmaceuticals were easily available in the country.

It was later that some daring industrialists attempted to set up some industries especially cotton textiles, jute in and around big cities like Bombay, Calcutta, and Madras, and an iron factory at Bokaro in Bengal. The Tata Iron and Steel Company came into existence in 1907. It was only during the First and Second World Wars that the establishing of more industries were encouraged and some protection granted by the then Government.

After Independence, the outlook of Government showed a complete change, and need for *self-sufficiency* in the field of industrial development was realized. So far, the industries had been much dominated by the private entrepreneurs whose main objective was the maximum profits. But now the private sector, which for long had been acclaimed as the backbone of the democratic or capitalistic system of production and the only way of the economic advancement of a country, was viewed from another angle. The growing monopolies and evils of capitalism necessitated the development and **nationalisation** of public utility, heavy and key industries including defiance industries. This gave impetus to the growth of public sector which simply means "ownership and management of the undertaking by the Government". Hence, Government-owned industries were started to give practical meaning to the *welfare* state.

India has adopted a socialistic pattern of society. Its economy is *mixed economy* where neither states not individuals control all the aspects of **national economy**. The industrial policy is so framed as to develop the private sector and the public sector side by side. They are not competitive but complementary. We need as much of one as that of the other. Hence, the public sector should not be made to grow at the cost of the private sector. There should be happy co-ordination in the two with some security to the private sector.

The field of management which deals with industry is called the *Industrial Sector*. Industrialisation is a process responsible for widening of capital and achieving rapid economic developments of the country.

Helpful vocabulary:

privet sector	القطاع الخاص
public sector	القطاع العام
finished goods	سِلَع مصنَّعة
the then government	الحكومة في ذلك الوقت
appreciable attempts	محاولات جادة ، محاولات ذات شأن
in spite of the fact that	بالرغم من حقيقة أن
daring industrialists	صناعيون جريئون
cotton textiles	منسوجات قطنية
to come into existence	يظهر الى حيز الوجود
self - sufficiency	اكتفاء ذاتي
capitalistic system of production	النظام الرأسمالي للإنتاج
viewed from another angle	نُظر إاليه من زاوية أخرى
heavy and key industries	الصناعات الثقيلة والأساسية
defiance industries	الصناعات الحربية ، الصناعات الدفاعية
welfare state	دولة الرخاء
government –owned industries	صناعة تملكها الحكومة
mixed economy	اقتصاد مختلط
national economy	الاقتصاد القومي
side by side	جنبا الى جنب معاً
at the cost of	على حساب
industrial sector	القطاع الصناعي
sophisticated machines	آلات معقدة
sole proprietorship	الملكية الفردية
at priority	أولا، قبل كل شيء
for the welfare of the public	من أجل الرخاء العام

Exercise 1. *Translate the previous passage into Arabic.*

Exercise 2. *Fill in this table with the suitable English derivatives whenever possible, and write down the Arabic equivalents of all the words.*

Verb		Noun		Adjective	
English	Arabic	English	Arabic	English	Arabic
compare					
		market			
				recent	
finish					
		fact			
				appreciable	
make					
		war			
				dominated	
exist					
		protection			
				economic	
grant					
				practical	
		sector			
realize					
		security		competitive	
grow					
				rapid	

Exercise 3. *Translate these terms:*

balance of payments	——————	bank advances	——————
balance sheet	——————	bank balance	——————
balance sheet audit	——————	bank note	——————
balance sheet forecast	——————	bank charges	——————
bank account	——————	bank check	——————

UNIT 18

INDESTRIAL SITUATION AND ITS NATURE

In an industrial situation, various factors like men, machines, material, money, methods, and management interact for a creative activity. Raw material enters the factory and is turned out in as saleable finished or semi-finished product .The following types of people are generally found carrying out an Industrial Activity:

1. **Unskilled workers**. Such workers carry out the manual work sweeping, clearing, watch and ward etc

2. **Semi-skilled workers**. Such workers operate the conventional type of machinery and carry out other operations, which do not require high skill.

3. **Skilled workers**. These workers operate all types of machines conventional as well was sophisticated .They have specialised training and can read and interpret drawings and blue prints.

4. **Men with technical competency**. They have undergone specialised vocation and training and have technical competency of a higher order .They can design, develop, and implement. Such persons are competent to supervise the work of skilled and semi-skilled workers

5. **Managerial personnel.** These persons have managerial talents and hold top positions in an organization. They are expert in their respective fields of management *viz.* production, personnel, sales, finance etc. They are concerned with directing, planning, and control.

Perfect coordination of all factors of production is necessary in order to achieve the targets of the factory .Every industrial enterprise has the following main objectives:

1. Optimum utilization of resource.
2. Standardization of products.
3. Specialization in the field of production.
4. To produce with quality
5. Stepping up production with the given resources
6. Welfare of the personnel engaged in the society as a whole.

MANAGEMENT OF MEN, MATERIALS, AND MACHINES

The success of an industrial enterprise depends largely upon the co-ordination of the factors of production *viz.* men materials, and machines. *Profitability* of an organization depends upon how much it in able to coordinate these factors .The secret of progress of an organization lies in its correlating efficiently and effectively the factors of production.

Helpful vocabulary:

creative activity	نشاط خلّاق
raw material	المادة الخام
saleable product	منتوج قابل للبيع
unskilled workers	عمال غير مَهَرَة
manual work	عمل يدوي
semi-skilled workers	عمال نصف مَهَرَة
skilled workers	عمال مَهَرَة
technical competency	مقدرة فنية ، مقدرة تِقْنِيّة
of a higher order	ذات مستوى أعلى
managerial personnel	الموظفون الإداريون
top positions	مناصب عُلْيا
perfect coordination	تنسيق كامل
industrial enterprise	مشروع صناعي
stepping up production	زِيَأْدَة الإنتاج
utilization of resources	تسخير الموارد
standardization of products	تعيير المنتوجات
factors of production	عوامل الإنتاج
to be taken into consideration	يُؤْخذ بعين الإعتبار
aptitude tests	اختبارات الاستعداد ، اختبارات القابلية
working conditions	ظروف العمل
financial incentives	حوافز مالية
safety measures	إجراءات السلامة
chances of promotions	فرص الترقيات
to the minimum	إلى الحد الأدنى
management of materials	إدارة المواد

Exercise 1. *Translate the previous passage into Arabic.*

Exercise 2. *Fill in this table with the suitable English derivatives whenever possible, and write down the Arabic equivalents of all the words.*

Verb		Noun		Adjective	
English	Arabic	English	Arabic	English	Arabic
		situation			
interact					
				general	
		product			
				clear	
		skill			
sweep				conventional	
watch		control			
operate				necessary	
train		profitability			
				effective	
plan					
		security			
				able	
direct					

Exercise 3. Translate these terms:

bank confirmation	_____	bank debit	_____
bank consortium	_____	bank disclosure	_____
bank credit	_____	bank draft	_____
bank currency	_____	bank discount	_____
bank deposits	_____	bank group	_____

UNIT 19

MANAGEMENT AS A PROFESSION

The word profession has been defined by various persons. The dictionary meaning of a profession is a 'calling which one professes to have acquired specialised knowledge which is used either in instructing, guiding, or advising others. Hodge and Johnson have defined the term profession "as a vocation requiring some significant body of knowledge that is applied with high degree of consistency in the service of some relevant segment of society". *Professionalism* requires a body of codified knowledge which can be taught and which can be applied with some degree of university. We shall give below the important features of a profession, and in the light of those features, determine whether management is a profession or not.

Main Characteristics of a profession

The late justice Brand of the Supreme Court of U.S.A enumerated the following peculiar characteristics of a profession as distinguished from other occupations.

1. It requires special knowledge and technical skill.
2. It is pursued largely for others and not merely for one's self.

3. It is an occupation in which the amount of financial return is not the accepted measure of success. Modern writers regard the following as other characteristics of profession.

4. There should be a code of conduct to guide the activities of the members of the profession.

5. There should be formalized methods of acquiring that knowledge.

6. There should be some formal organization to regular the behavior of members.

7. It should have enough membership to serve the society efficiently.

8. Its members should accept the obligation to contribute to the advancement of standards and to the education of the oncoming aspirants.

9. There should be adequate communication among members for purposes of maintaining membership cohesiveness and membership development.

10. There should be a bond of trust between those who profess the profession and their clients.

11. There should be rigid rules and standards of qualification for the entrance of newcomers into the profession.

2. It should build up an image of an independent agent.
If the above criteria are to be rigidly applied, management cannot be called a profession. Hodge and Johnson write: "Management does not at present meet the requirements and is not properly classified as a profession."

Helpful vocabulary:

managment as a profession	الأدارة كَمِهنة
body of knowledge	رصيد معرفي
with high degree of consistency	بدرجة عالية من الاتّساقِ
in the service of	في خدمة
in the light of	في ضوء
financial return	العائد المالي
measure of success	مقياس النجاح
code of conduct	ميثاق السلوك
formalized methods	طرق محددة
obligation to contribute	الإلتزام بالمساهمة
entrance of new comers	دخول أعضاء جدد
standards of qualifications	معايير المؤهلات
rigidly applied	مطبقة بدقة
professionalization of management	تمهين الادارة ، اعتبار الإدارة مهنة
a leading management authority	خبير بارز في الادارة
licensing mangers	ترخيص الإداريين ، إجازة الإداريين
bound to lead to	لا بُدَّ أن يؤدي إلى
access to management	الوصول إلى الإدارةِ
ups and downs	تقلُّبات
backed by	مدعومة بِـ
management principles	مبادئ الإدارة
moral climate	المناخ الأخلاقي
growing awareness	إدراك متزايد
management consultants	مستشارون إداريون
self – made managers	إداريون عصاميون

Exercise 1. *Translate the previous passage into Arabic.*

Exercise 2. *Fill in this table with the suitable English derivatives whenever possible, and write down the Arabic equivalents of all the words.*

Verb		Noun		Adjective	
English	Arabic	English	Arabic	English	Arabic
mean					
		profession			
				various	
advise					
apply					
		service			
				special	
determine					
				universal	
give					
		number			
				formal	
require					
				adequate	
		behavior			
guide					
				clear	
		standard			
disturb					
				evident	

Exercise 3. *Translate these terms:*

bank loan _____   best buy _____

bank pass-book _____   best price _____

bank statement _____   best seller _____

bank transfer _____   bid price _____

barter agreement _____   blacklist _____

UNIT 20

INDUSTRIAL RELATIONS

Industrial Relations is a combination of various social sciences the cumulative effect of which is to grease the wheels of Industry and society.

Sound Industrial Relations can only be based on human relations, and good human relations dictate that human beings should be treated humanly, which includes respect for *human dignity*, fair dealing and concern for the human beings' physical and social needs. Industrial Relations is also concerned with determination of wages and conditions of employment.

Industrial Relations and *human relations* are distinctly two indispensable factors in Industry , one depending on the other .We can have good industrial relations in an industry, but dad human relations in the same establishment and vice versa. Good industrial relations provide the necessary background for good human relations.

In any undertaking, good relations between the management and workers depend upon the degree of mutual confidence which can be established. This, in turn, depends upon the recognition by the employees of the goodwill and *integrity of the management* in the day- today handling of questions which are of **mutual concern**.

The first requisite for the development of good industrial relations is a good **labour policy**. The aim of such a policy should be to secure the best possible co-operation of the employees. Every employee should have the opportunity to contribute not only his services, but his suggestions and ideas also towards the common effort.

The basic needs of an industrial worker are freedom from fear, **security of employment**, and freedom from want. Adequate food, better health, clothing, and housing are human requirements. The human heart harbours secret pride and invariably responds to courtesy and kindness just as it revolts to tyranny and fear. An environment where the employee is contented with his job, assured of a bright future, and provided with his basic needs in life means an atmosphere of good industrial relations.

Two-fold objectives of good **industrial relations** are to preserve industrial pace and to secure *industrial co-operation*. If we have to establish industrial peace, the workers must be assured of fair wages, good conditions of work, reasonable working hours, holidays, and minimum amenities of life.

Helpful Vocabulary:

Industrial Relations	العلاقات الصناعية
cumulative effect	تأثير تراكمي
human dignity	الكرامة الإنسانية
fair dealing	المعاملة العادلة
and vice versa	والعكس بالعكس
indispensable factors	عوامل لا غنى عنها
mutual confidence	ثقة متبادلة
mutual concern	اهتمام متبادل
goodwill and integrity	النوايا الطيبة والنزاهة
labor policy	سياسة عُمَّالية
freedom from fear	التخلص من الخوف
security of employment	الأمن الوظيفي
freedom from want	التخلص من العَوَز
to respond to courtesy	يستجيب للمجاملة
contented with his job	راضٍ بوظيفته
basic needs	الحاجات الأساسية
industrial peace	السلام الصناعي
fair wages	أجور عادلة
effective coordination	تنسيق فَعَّال
harmonious atmosphere	جوّ منسجم
trade unions	الاتحادات الحرفية
minimum requirements	المتطلبات الدنيا
on the part of	من جانب
labor laws	قوانين العمل
prevention of accidents	منع الحوادث

Exercise 1. *Translate the previous passage into Arabic.*

Exercise 2. *Fill in this table with the suitable English derivatives whenever possible, and write down the Arabic equivalents of all the words.*

Verb		Noun		Adjective	
English	Arabic	English	Arabic	English	Arabic
fascinate					
		study			
				cumulative	
		discussion			
				based	
		respect			
contribute					
		relation			
				mutual	
respond					
		industry			
foster					
		question			
define					
		employee			
co-ordinate					
		labour			

Exercise 3. Translate these terms:

bill of lading	————————	bill receivable	————————
bill of health	————————	bill retired	————————
bill of sales	————————	black bourse	————————
bill of sight	————————	black market	————————
bill payable	————————	blank check	————————

UNIT 21

AN OVERVIEW OF MANAGERIAL FINANCE

What role does "finance" play within the firm? What specific tasks are assigned to the financial staff, and what tools and techniques are available to it for improving the firm's performance? On a broader scale, what is the role of finance in the U.S economy, and how can financial management be used to further our national goals? As we shall see, proper **financial management** within the firm will help the business provide better products at lower prices to its customers, pay higher wages and salaries to its workers and managers, and still provide greater returns to the investors who put up the capital needed to form and then operate the business. Since the economy – both national and world –consists of customers, employees, and investors, sound financial management contributes both to individual well-being and to the well-being of the population.

The **financial manager** must plan for the acquisition and use of funds so as to maximize the value of the firm .In short, financial managers make decisions about alternative sources and uses of funds. This definition involves several important activities:

1. *Forecasting and planning.* The financial manager must interact with other executives as they jointly look ahead and lay the plans which will shape the **future position** of the firm.

2. *Major investment and financing decision.* On the basis long - run plans, the financial manager must raise the capital needed to support growth .A successful firm usually achieves a high rate of growth in sales, which requires increased investments by the firm in the plant, equipment, and **current assets** necessary for the production of goods and services. The financial manager must help determine the optimal rate of sales growth, and he or she must rank alternative projects available to the firm. He or she must help decide on the specific investments to be made as well as on the alternative sources and forms of funds for financing these investments. Decisions must be made about the use of internal versus external funds, the use of debt versus owners' equity, and the use of long-term versus short-term financing.

3. *Control.* The financial manager must interact with executives in other parts of these businesses to help the firm operate as efficiently as possible. All **business decisions** have financial implications, and all managers –financial and otherwise –need to take this into account. For example, marketing decision affect sales growth, which in turn changes *investment requirements*.

Helpful vocabulary:

managerial finance	المالية الإدارية
managerial perspective	منظور إداري
firm's performance	أداء الشركة
financial management	الإدارة المالية
individual well-being	رفاهية الفرد
financial manger	المدير المالي
alternative sources	المصادر البديلة
future position	الوضع المستقبلي
rate of growth in sales	معدل نمو المبيعات
long-run plans	الخطط بعيدة المدى
alternative projects	مشاريع بديلة
financing investments	تمويل الإستثمارات
financial implications	مُتَضَّمنات مالية
marketing decisions	قرارات التسويق
sales growth	زيادت المبيعات ، نمو المبيعات
to take into account	يأخذ في الأعتبار
inventory policy	سياسة الجَرْد
plant capacity utilization	إستغلال طاقة المصنع
capital markets	أسواق رأس المال
to get the most out of	يستفيد منها الإستفادة القصوى
optimal manner	الشكل الأمثل
financial institutions	مؤسسات مالية
investment portfolios	الحقائب الاستثمارية
legal aspects	الجوانب القانونية
transfers of funds	تحويلات الأرصدة

Exercise 1. *Translate the previous passage into Arabic.*

Exercise 2. *Fill in this table with the suitable English derivatives whenever possible, and write down the Arabic equivalents of all the words.*

	Verb		Noun		Adjective
English	Arabic	English	Arabic	English	Arabic
improve					
				specific	
		staff			
				low	
invest					
		manager			
help					
				financial	
		capital			
interact					
				internal	
need					
		change			
				separate	
grow					
		relation			
				legal	
		trade			

Exercise 3. *Translate these terms:*

block grant	——————	bonus share	——————
board of directors	——————	bonus issue	——————
board of guardians	——————	bonus account	——————
board of trade	——————	book loss	——————
board of trustees	——————	book of invitatory	——————

99

UNIT 22

MEASUREMENT OF EXPENES

The pattern and volume of operative and administrative expenses are determined by the asset structure, sales, and production pattern, whereas the pattern of financial expenses like *interest* costs is determined by capital structure.

Expenses are flow of assets inclusive of working assets out of firm in the process of creation of income. They arise as the resources of business are utilised for the creation of revenues. All expenses must be in the form of cash. Even the so-called *non-cash expenses* were cash expenses at one time. Expenses are measured by the amount of decrease in assets or increase in liabilities in the process of earning income.

As in the case of measurement of income, the consideration to be given to factors like timing are implicit in the case of measurement of expenses also.

The expenses are to be recognized and associated closely to the period when the corresponding incomes are identified. The problem of measurement of expenses becomes complex (*a*) When the benefits of a single outlay are received over a number of **accounting periods**, and (*b*) the interval between cash outlay and the expiration of acquired assets or services is longer .

Some of the problems in recognizing the expenses under the assumption of uncertainty are:

a) *Changes in the price level,* which affects the depreciation charge (the method of **depreciation** itself affects the volume and timing of expenses). One of the arguments for charging depreciation on the basis of historical cost is this: why should the present generation pay for the future generations? Similarly, the other argument is this: how could the present generation drive the benefit of an investment made at lower prices by the past generation?

B) *Inventory Valuation Method.* Many firms tend to adopt LIFO to alleviate distortion and reduce incidence of income-tax during the ties of rising prices.

c) *Valuation of Receivables.* Income measurement is distorted if the prices are changing fast and there is a gap between the time of sale and actual realisation of **cash receivables**.

d) *The interest charges* etc., to be paid on the liabilities acquired or contracted at the time when the price levels were different.

Helpful vocabulary:

operative expenses	نفقات التشغيل
administrative expenses	نفقات إدارية
production pattern	نمط الإنتاج
interest cost	تكاليف الفوائد
creation of revenues	إيجاد المداخيل
non-cash expenses	نفقات غير نقدية
process of earning income	عملية كسب الدخلِ
measurement of expenses	قياس النفقات
accounting periods	فترات المحاسبية
price level	مستوى الأسعار
present generation	الجيل الحالي
inventory valuation method	أسلوب تقييم البضاعة الموجودة
L I F O (= Last in ,first out.)	البضائع الداخلة أخيراً تباع أولاً
Valuation of Receivables	تثمين حسابات المدينين
independent of	مستقل عن ، غير معتمد على
net assets	صافي الأصول
uninsured property	ممتلكات غير مؤمنة
increase in assets	زيادة في الأصول
law suit	قضية قانونية
capital gains	مكاسب رأسمالية
capital losses	خسائر رأسماليه
gains and losses	مكاسب و خسائر
profits and losses	أرباح و خسائر
operating profits	أرباح التشغيل
appropriation account	حساب توزيع الأرباح

Exercise 1. *Translate the previous passage into Arabic.*

Exercise 2. *Fill in this table with the suitable English derivatives whenever possible, and write down the Arabic equivalents of all the words.*

	Verb		Noun		Adjective	
English	**Arabic**	**English**	**Arabic**	**English**	**Arabic**	
		pattern				
				operative		
utilize						
		structure				
				financial		
measure						
		sale				
				single		
recognize						
		generation				
depreciate						
		argument				
				temporary		
represent						
		gain				
prefer						
		loss				

Exercise 3. Translate these terms:

book of terms	_____	branch account	_____
book profit	_____	branch bank	_____
book value	_____	branch manager	_____
bottom price	_____	branch office	_____
bought day book	_____	bridging loan	_____

UNIT 23

THE ECONOMIC FUNCTIONS AND GOALS OF THE PUBLIC SECTOR

The basic economic problem of *scarcity* provides a logical point of departure for the study of public finance .The resources available to any society are limited in their ability to produce economic goods by both quantitative and **qualitative constraints**. *Land*, which may be defined generally as natural resources, is limited in quantity by the geographical area of the nation and by the magnitude of raw material deposits within this land area. Moreover, natural resources vary in quality among nations. *Labor* faces quantitative constraints as a productive resource through the numerical size and age distribution of the society's population and qualitative limitations through such determinants as the prevailing ethical, health, and educational standards of the society. *Capital* is limited in quantity by the society's past capital formation behavior and in quality by the relationship of its capital stock to the prevailing state of technology.

This limited supply of the **productive resources** available to a society leads to the *allocation function* of economics. The unlimited eescope of aggregate human wants, along with the limited resources which produce the economic goods capable of satisfying these wants, make it necessary to allocate the scarce resources among alternative uses. An infinite or unlimited quantity of **economic goods** cannot be produced. When certain goods are produced with the scarce resources, the opportunities to produce other goods are foregone , assuming there is full employment of resources.

Thus, an *economic system* must exist to determine the pattern of production, that is, to answer these questions: what economic goods should be produced, and in what quantities ought they to be produced? The allocation function possesses an additional important dimension: it must be concerned with the *institutional means* through which the allocation decisions are processed. This requirement establishes the link between the basic **economic problems** of scarcity and the study of public finance, since modern society offers two institutions through which the decisions of the allocation branch of economics may be made – the *market* and the *government*. The market institution is designated the *private sector*, and government institution the *public sector*.

The forces of supply and demand and the *price mechanism*, as determined by consumer sovereignty and producer profit motives, characterize private sector **resource allocation** public sector allocation, on the other hand, is accomplished through the revenue and expenditure activates of governmental budgeting.

Helpful vocabulary:

public sector	القطاع العام
problem of scarcity	مشكلة النُّدْرَة
resources available	الموارد المتاحة
quantitative and qualitative constraints	ضوابط كمية ونوعية
raw material deposits	مخزونات المواد الخام
productive resources	موارد إنتاجية
age distribution	التوزيع العُمْريّ
capital stock	أسهم رأس المال
human wants	الحاجات البشرية
full employment of resources	الاستخدام الكامل للموارد
additional dimension	بُعْدٌ إضافي
institutional means	وسيلة مؤسَّسِيَّة
market institution	مؤسسةُ السُّوقِ
forces of supply and demand	قوى العرض والطلب
price mechanism	آلية السِّعْر
consumer sovereignty	سيادة المستهلك
producer profit motives	دوافع الربح لدى المنتج
resource allocation	تخصيص الموارد
that is	أيْ، وبعبارة أخرى
mixed economy	اقتصاد مختلط
wealth distribution	توزيع الثروة
capital utilization	تشغيل رأس المال
national economy	الاقتصاد القومي

Exercise 1. *Translate the previous passage into Arabic.*

Exercise 2. *Fill in this table with the suitable English derivatives whenever possible, and write down the Arabic equivalents of all the words.*

	Verb		Noun		Adjective
English	Arabic	English	Arabic	English	Arabic
		quantity			
prevail					
				available	
		size			
				productive	
form					
vary					
		reality			
				infinite	
				scarce	
		orientation			
allocate					
				national	
				neutral	
refer					
		function			

Exercise 3. *Translate these terms:*

brokerage firm	_____	budget manual	_____
broker's market	_____	budget review	_____
budget account	_____	budget surplus	_____
budget committee	_____	bulk sale	_____
budget controller	_____	burden of losses	_____

UNIT 24

ORGANIZATIONAL
THEORY

Since the 1920s, organisation theory has developed rapidly .Its primary purpose as an academic study is to understand and explain the behavior and functioning of organisations. However , the reason for the *diversion of resources* towards it lies in the hope that it will lead to the creation of new more effective organisational forms. The similarity between large private administrative organisations and the bureaucracies (*see* VII) of the stare has meant that much of the work of organisational theorists is relevant to public administration.

The relevance is particular apparent to those public sector organisations that are concerned with the provision of goods and services – for example, *the nationalized industries* as well as departments such as Health and Social Security , and Employment The Fulton Committee (*see* VI) with its emphasis on the importance of management principles to the administrative **civil service** generally may be seen as an acknowledgement of the connection of the theories to the operation of all public sector administration.

In many fields such as organization and methods, manpower

planning, and operational research, developments in the public sector have paralleled similar innovations in the private sector.

It must always be borne in mind that public administration operates within a **political environment**, the most obvious effect of which is that its "goals" – aims and objectives – are more widely based and subject to more frequent change. In addition, the following constraints on the application of theory should be borne in mind.

(a) The nature of the basic administrative problem which varies substantially from the basic problem in *private business* .This problem has two basic elements:

(i) Administration must accord with the social and economic environment;

(ii) It must provide that environment with services needed by society if it is to function and progress.

(b) In particular, government disposes of coercive powers, which do not arise in the private sector, and, partly for this reason, administrative **decision-making** is bound by rules of consultation, objection, and appeal, which have no parallel in the private sector.

(c) Government undertakes or sponsors speculative ventures, e.g., in technology, which have no close equivalents.

Helpful vocabulary:

organization theory	نظرية المنظمات
diversion of resources	تحويل الموارد
lie in the hope that	يأتي على أمل أنَّ
organisational theorists	مُنَظِّرو التنظيم
particularly apparent	ظاهر بوجه خاصّ
provision of goods and services	توفير السِّلع والخدمات
nationalized industries	الصناعات المؤممة
acknowledgement of the connection	إقرار بالصلة
manpower planning	تخطيط القوى البشرية
operational research	بحث العمليات
subject to change	مُعَرَّض للتغيُّر
varies substantially from	تختلف كثيراً عن
accord with	تتوافقْ مع
bound by rules of consultation	محدود بأحكام التشاور
objection and appeal	الإعتراض والاستئناف
have no parallel	لا نظير لها
market innovation	مستجدات السوق
public administration	الإدارة العامة
public welfare	الرفاهي العام، الخير العام
quantifying goal	تكميم الأهداف
demands of society	مطالب المجتمع
slow reaction	رد الفعل البطيء
faculty of initiative	موهبة المبادرة
overlapping of functions	تداخل المهامّ، تداخل الوظائف

Exercise 1. *Translate the previous passage into Arabic.*

Exercise 2. *Fill in this table with the suitable English derivatives whenever possible, and write down the Arabic equivalents of all the words.*

Verb		Noun		Adjective	
English	Arabic	English	Arabic	English	Arabic
		purpose			
		resource			
		effect			
		organization			
acknowledge					
				national	
		aim			
mach					
		constraint			
				private	
market					
				economic	
compete					
		theorist			
				frequent	
sponsor					
		public			
				consequent	

Exercise 3. *Translate these terms:*

Bureau of Custom	_____	business ethics	_____
Bureau of Labor Statistics	_____	business entity	_____
Bureau of the Budget	_____	business enterprise	_____
Bureau of the Census	_____	business expansion	_____
business cycle	_____	business publication	_____

UNIT 25

INTERNATIONAL BANKING

Cleary ,the structure of international banking has developed and changed in response to the needs of the world economy and , over the past decade , its rate of growth has been faster than at any time in its history. for British international banks, the extensive network of banking correspondents built up over many decades has been maintained – the Midland Bank alone has a working relationship with some 20,000 correspondent banking outlets in over 120 countries throughout the world. These old established ties, based on mutual trust and respect, have proved, and are proving, to be a powerful springboard on which to base fresh initiatives for meeting the now challenges of a changing world. Such developments may be clearly seen in the closer ties now being forged between British banks and other **financial institutions** and their counterparts in the Middle East.

As we are all acutely aware, the scope of international business has widened considerably in recent years. Originally , the principal function of many grouping and associations was to provide international **merchant banking services**, and, in particular, medium-term loans, either directly or through joint subsidiaries. Although this still remains a typical operation, international activities have now been extended at both the long and short ends of the lending business, while such specialist services as export financing, leasing, and factoring have become increasingly important. British banks have, in the past, played a less significant role in Eurobond business than in the shorter term Euro-currency markets, but issues of bonds by multinational and other companies are being increasingly sponsored and placed by British banks.

Foreign Exchange Business

Despite the problems raised by the possibility of large fluctuations in exchange rates, the present system of floating rates has worked much better than was ever anticipated. Indeed, currency crises of the severity of those that occurred several times before the general adoption of floating exchange rates in 1973 have so far been avoided. This is particularly notable in view of the wide differences in **rates of inflation** in major countries, the unsettling influence of the shift in holdings of large balances to oil producers and the necessary recycling process, and the constant threat of a deeper plunge into international recession some uncertainties have, of course , occurred from time to time in foreign exchange markets, but the freer movement of market rates has proved to be an adequate safety valve in dissipating destabilizing forces when these have built up. Heavy speculative losses in foreign exchange dealing been incurred by some market operators, but , on a general view, monetary authorities have been able to pay less attention to a given parity and to concentrate their attention on other aims of economic policy.

Helpful vocabulary:

international banking	أعمال مصرفية دولية
world economy	الاقتصاد العالمي
rate of growth	معدل النمو
international banks	مصاريف دولية
established ties	روابط راسخة ، روابط وثيقة
mutual trust	ثقة متبادلة
financial institutions	مؤسسات مالية
banking services	خدمات مَصْرفية
medium –term loans	قروض متوسّطة الأجل
joint subsidiaries	فروع متضامنة
specialist services	خدمات متخصصة
export financing	تمويل التصدير
Euro- currency markets	أسواق العملات الاوروبية
Euro- bond business	تجارة السندات الأوروبية
fluctuation in exchange rates	تذبذب في أسعار الصرف
floating rates	أسعار معوَّمة
rates of inflation	معدلات التضخم
oil producers	منتجو النفط
unsettling influence	تأثير غير مستقر
international recession	ركود دولي، انكماش (اقتصادي) دولي
foreign exchange markets	أسواق صرف العملات الأجنبية
destabilizing forces	قوى باعثة على عدم الاستقرار
heavy speculative losses	خسائر متوقعة ثقيلة
central banks	مصارف مركزية
tighter supervision	مراقبة أدقّ

Exercise 1. *Translate the previous passage into Arabic.*

Exercise 2. *Fill in this table with the suitable English derivatives whenever possible, and write down the Arabic equivalents of all the words.*

Verb		Noun		Adjective	
English	Arabic	English	Arabic	English	Arabic
		structure			
maintain					
		economy			
				recent	
		growth			
				direct	
extend					
		activity			
				short	
remain					
		initiative			
				long	
		example			
				considerable	
occur					
				typical	
		exchange			
anticipate					
		profit			

Exercise 3. *Translate these terms:*

buying order	——————	by tender	——————
buying department	——————	by-product	——————
buying agent	——————	cable credit	——————
buying office	——————	cable transfer	——————
bylaws	——————	calendar year	——————

UNIT 26

MULTINATIONAL COMPANIES

Consider a manager of a medium-sized American auto parts manufacturer who must decide whether to expand production capacity to meet growing demand in Eastern Europe. The capital budgeting committee of the **board of directors** has asked her to evaluate the feasibility of opening a manufacturing plant in Poland. Our manager would need to be familiar with most areas of international finance.

First, she would need to ascertain *political and credit risk factors* relevant to the investment. What are the relevant tax laws and how might they change over the life of the investment? What is the potential for labor strife, riots, and military intervention? Are there restrictions on imports and exports, and how likely are they to change? What are the relevant health, safety, and environmental regulations, and how are they likely to evolve? What are the **commercial laws** and customs associated with accounts payable and accounts receivable? What are the costs and the availability of banking services? Are there any foreign exchange restrictions, and are they likely to change in the future? After ascertaining the relevant risk factors, our manager would have to estimate both the cost of controlling these risks and any unavoidable losses.

Second, our hypothetical manager would have to analyze the potential exposure of the company to *currency risk*. What is the exchange rate for converting Polish currency into dollars? What are the exchange rates between Polish currency and the currencies of other European countries that the plant might export to? What are the forecasts for currency exchange rates in the future? What instruments and techniques are available for hedging these currency risks? Upon completing an assessment of these risk factors, our manager would then have to estimate the *costs of hedging*, along with a range of net present values in dollars for the investment.

Third, our manager would have to *investigate interest rates* and *inflation rates* in all relevant countries. In which countries should financing be obtained? How much debt and how much equity? What maturity is most appropriate? Should the company obtain a Eurocurrency loan? At what rate will **operating costs** increase? Will competitors' prices increase as rapidly? Having addressed these questions, the manager would also have to assess the likelihood and availability of refinancing both in the United States and abroad.

Clearly, *multinational business* is not for the fainthearted or the uneducated. Nevertheless, companies will always be eager to confront the costs and complexities of multinational business when the potential rewards exceed the expenses and expenses and risks.

Helpful vocabulary:

multinational companies	شركات متعددة الجنسيات
auto - parts manufacturer	صانع قطع غيار السيارات
production capacity	الطاقة الإنتاجية
growing demand	طلب متزايد
capital budgeting committee	لجنة ميزانية رأس المال
board of directors	هيئة المديرين ، مجلس المديرين
manufacturing plant	مصنع إنتاج
relevant tax laws	القوانين الضريبية ذات العلاقة
restrictions on imports	قيود على الواردات
commercial laws and customs	القوانين التجارية والرسوم الجمركية
risk factors	عوامل المخاطرة
unavoidable losses	خسائر محتومة
hypothetical manager	مدير افتراضي
exchange rate	أسعار الصرف
interest rates	أسعار الفائدة
inflation rates	معدلات التضخم
operating costs	تكاليف التشغيل
competitors' prices	أسعار المنافسين
be in no position to	ليس في وضع يمكنه من أن
deutsche mark	المارك الألماني
trade credit	تسليف تجاري
prior to delivery	قبل التسليم
forecasts of rates	التنبؤات بالأسعار

Exercise 1. *Translate the previous passage into Arabic.*

Exercise 2. *Fill in this table with the suitable English derivatives whenever possible, and write down the Arabic equivalents of all the words.*

	Verb		Noun		Adjective
English	**Arabic**	**English**	**Arabic**	**English**	**Arabic**
		size			
decide					
open					
cost					
				available	
analyze					
		exchange			
				present	
estimate					
		forecast			
export					
				feasible	
		reward			
import					
assess					
		question			
				familiar	

Exercise 3. *Translate these terms:*

call deposit	_____	capital amount	_____
call for tenders	_____	capital asset	_____
call loan	_____	capital budget	_____
call money	_____	capital consumption	_____
capital account	_____	capital costs	_____

UNIT 27

URO-CURRENCY MARKETS

Euro-currencies have, for some years, become increasingly important as a source of international finance. The development of this market has helped to bring about a vast expansion in international trade and, more recently, has provided a convenient **method of financing** for medium and longer term investment. Such medium-term lending, mainly undertaken by international and consortium banks, has rapidly filled the previous gap between the short-term Euro-dollar market and the longer term Eurobond market and has encroached to some extent on the long end of the market.

With British domestic banks, foreign banks in London , and the consortium banks specially established in London all actively engaging in this market, London soon became the main center for Euro-currency business. It has retained this position, and it accounts for more than 40 per cent of the world market. Estimates differ as to the size of the Euro-currency market, but it is generally reckoned that London is responsible for nearly one half of the Euro-currency business done by European bank. The Bank for International Settlements put the size of Euro-currency business at the end of 1974 at $220,000m. or $77,000m. net of double-counting as a result of **interbank re-depositing.** The estimates suggest that the market has already doubled in two years and has quadrupled in five years. Including the foreign currency activates of banks in places outside the European reporting area, the net size of the Euro- currency market was estimated at about $210.000m. as at the end of 1974 and has probably risen somewhat since then, though at a slower rate than in 1973 and 1974.

Over the past two years, the most important factor behind the growth of the Euro-currency market has been the sharp rise in the price of oil and the consequent transfer of **foreign currency balances** into the hands of the oil-producing countries. In 1974 alone, new funds injected into the market from this source amounted to about $24.000m, while several thousand million dollars were also deposited by oil companies.

The problem involved in recycling such vast sums of money was highlighted at first by the natural reluctance of holders of these balances to deposit their funds other than at very short terms. This had especially strong repercussions on smaller **banking organizations** and on banks which had already been heavy takers of Euro-funds. This led for a time to a much wider spread of rates between short and longer term deposits than hitherto. It also resulted in a more complicated tiered system of rates which reflected the changed credit rating of banks in particular countries as well as individual banks, depending on such things their size and existing involvement in the market.

Helpful vocabulary:

Euro-currency markets	أسواق العملات الأوربية
international finance	تمويل دَولي
international trade	تجارة دولية
medium-term lending	إقراض متوسط الأجل
consortium banks	مصارف متحدة
Eurobond market	سوق السندات الأوروبية
domestic banks	مصارف محلية
interbank re-depositing	إعادة الإيداع عبر البنوك
net size	الحجم الصافي
sharp rise	ارتفاع الحادّ
oil companies	شركات النفط
to deposit funds	يودع الأموالِ
to attract deposits	يجذب الودائع
general disquiet	القلق العام
recycling process	عملية إعادة التدوير
atmosphere of apprehension	جو من الترقب، جو من الترقب الحَذِر
substantial losses	خسائر كبيرة
monetary authorities	سلطات نقدية
to regain confidences	يستعيد الثقة
stabilizing response	استجابة مُطَمْئِنة

Exercise 1. *Translate the previous passage into Arabic.*

Exercise 2. *Fill in this table with the suitable English derivatives whenever possible, and write down the Arabic equivalents of all the words.*

	Verb		Noun		Adjective
English	**Arabic**	**English**	**Arabic**	**English**	**Arabic**
provide					
		factor			
				sharp	
include					
		year			
				near	
		place			
retain					
				heavy	
		market			
inject					
		trade			
				vast	
		deposit			
				willing	
recycle					
		process			

Exercise 3. *Translate these terms:*

capital gain	——————	capital market	——————
capital gearing	——————	capital owned	——————
capital increase	——————	capital reserve	——————
capital decrease	——————	capital shares	——————
capital loss	——————	capital surplus	——————

123

UNIT 28

SUCCESSFUL INVESTING

Saving regularly and investing these savings wisely are the central purposes of personal financial planning, and they are essential to achieving financial security. One of the major tasks that you confront on the way to **financial independence**, therefore, is learning how to invest successfully; that is, to find the right balance of stock, interest-earning, and, perhaps , real estate investments that will provide growth and, at the same time, preserve your hard-earned savings.

The importance of proper diversification in achieving these goals on a long-team basis is immeasurable. Consider that between August and October of 1987 the **stock market** lost almost 28 percent of its value. While the market subsequently regained that drop, anyone who had all of his or her money in stocks during that period would have lost a tremendous amount of saving if, for some reason , that investor was forced to sell the holdings shortly after the downturn. However, people who have restricted their investments to safer money market funds and certificates of deposit (CDs) are barely keeping up with inflation – hardly a successful investment result.

Determining an appropriate investment allocation requires an evaluation and periodic review of your personal and **financial situation** including age, family status, income, income prospects, objectives , and personal preferences. Generally, the younger you are, the greater the investment risk you can afford to take in exchange for potentially achieving greater investment returns. A retiree, however, should generally opt for a less aggressive investment approach.

Of course, other matters may also influence your investment strategy. A retiree who has substantial income from a pension and **Social Security** can afford to take a greater degree of investment risk than someone who depends largely on personal saving for income. People who are uncomfortable with investment risk may be better suited for a relatively conservative portfolio, even though it offers less potential for growth than a more aggressive one.

Another factor that must be considered in the investment allocation and selection process is the relative attractiveness of various types of investments. This does not mean that you must shift your investments frequently to achieve financial success. In fact , it is usually the opposite: Buying and holding is a better course. However, you should periodically review your **portfolio** to ensure that your current investment mix is appropriate in light of prevailing market conditions as well as your.personal situation.

Helpful vocabulary:

Successful invest	الاستثمار الناجح
personal financial planning	تخطيط مالي شخصي
financial security	الأمن المالي
hard-earned savings	مدّخرات مكتسبة بصعوبة
proper diversification	تنويع مناسب
to regain the drop	يستعيد (قيمة) الانخفاض
stock market	سوق الأسهم
certificate of deposit (CDs)	شهادة إيداع
periodic review	مراجعة منتظمة
investment returns	عوائد استثمارية
in exchange for	مقابل
for some reason	لسبب ما
aggressive investment approach	نهج استثماري جريء
investment strategy	استراتيجية استثمارية
investment risk	مخاطر الاستثمار
relative attractiveness	جاذبية نسبية
investment mix	التشكيلة الاستثمارية
to outpace inflation	يسبق التضخم
average investor	المستثمر العادي
investment alternatives	بدائل استثمارية

Exercise 1. *Translate the previous passage into Arabic.*

Exercise 2. *Fill in this table with the suitable English derivatives whenever possible, and write down the Arabic equivalents of all the words.*

	Verb		Noun		Adjective
English	Arabic	English	Arabic	English	Arabic
		person			
		value			
force					
		age			
invest					
				relative	
		period			
				attractive	
drop					
		reason			
achieve					
		risk			
				opposite	
earn					
preserve					
		review			
help					

Exercise 3. *Translate these terms:*

capital tax	————	carriage paid	————
card index	————	carried down	————
cargo liner	————	carried forward	————
cargo value	————	cash account	————
carriage forward	————	cash advance	————

UNIT 29

CURRENT ACCOUNT

The *current account* is defined as including the value of trade in merchandise, service, investment income, and unilateral transfers. Merchandise is the obvious trade in tangible commodities. *Services* refers to trade in the services of factors of production: land, labor, and capital. Included in this category are travel and tourism, royalties, transportation costs, and insurance premiums. The payment for the services of physical capital, or the **return on investments**, is recorded in the vestment income account. The amounts of interest and dividends paid internationally are large and are growing rapidly as the world financial markets become more integrated.

The final component of the balance of payments includes unilateral transfers, like U.S foreign aid, gifts, and **retirement pensions**. The United States always records a large deficit on these items ,except for 1991, when several foreign countries transferred large sums of money to the United States to help pay for the expense of the war in the Mideast.

Figure 2.2 illustrates how the various account balances have changed over time. The merchandise and current account deficits of the

1980 were unprecedented. In Figure 2.1, line 71 shows that there was a current account surplus of $ 2.331 million in 1970 and a deficit of $ 151.215 million in 1997. The $155 billion current account deficit of 1997 is the sum of a $198 billion merchandise trade deficit, an $88 billion **services surplus**, a $5 billion investment income deficit, and a $ 39 billion transfers deficit. From 1955 to 1970, the United States ran a merchandise trade surplus. Following a $2 billion deficit in 1971, the merchandise account has been in deficit every year since, except 1973 and 1975. Even with this persistent merchandise trade deficit, U.S. earnings from foreign investments have had sizable surpluses so that the current account realized a surplus in the periods from 1973 to 1976 and from 1980 to 1981.

The balance of payments in figure 2.1 actually ends at line 64. Lines 65 to 71 are summaries drawn from Lines 1 to 64. We can draw a line in the **balance of payments** to sum the debit and credit items above that line. If we draw the line at the current account balance items ending with unilateral transfers (line 32), all the entries below that line account for financing the merchandise, services, investment income, and unilateral transfers (gifts); thus, the current account indicates whether a country is a net borrower from , or lender to, the rest of the world. A current account surplus implies that a country is running a net deficit below the line and that the country is a net lender to the rest of the world.

Helpful vocabulary:

current account	حسابٌ جارٍ
investment income	دخل الاستثمار
tangible commodities	سلع محسوسة
factors of production	عوامل الإنتاج
transportation costs	تكاليف النقل
insurance premiums	أقساط التأمين
unilateral transfers	تحويلات من جانب واحد
foreign aid	المعونة الأجنبية
retirement pensions	رواتب التقاعد
account balances	موازين المراجعة
current account deficits	عجز الحساب الجاري
current account surplus	فائض حساب الجاري
the sum of	مجموع
merchandise trade deficit	عجز تجارة البضائع
services surplus	فائض في الخدمات
investment income deficit	عجز في الدخل الاستثماري
merchandise account	الحساب التجاري
persistent deficit	عجز متواصل، عجز دائم
sizable surpluses	فوائض كبيرة
balance of payments	ميزان المدفوعات
debit items	بنود مدينة
credit items	بنود دائنة
net borrower	المستدين الصافي
net lender	الدائن الصافي

Exercise 1. *Translate the previous passage into Arabic.*

Exercise 2. *Fill in this table with the suitable English derivatives whenever possible, and write down the Arabic equivalents of all the words.*

	Verb		Noun		Adjective	
English	Arabic	English	Arabic	English	Arabic	
define						
		trade				
pay						
		service				
				rapid		
integrate						
		transfer				
				large		
		entry				
				unilateral		
illustrate						
		lender				
				actual		
market						
		borrower				
persist						
		world				

Exercise 3. *Translate these terms:*

cash asset	_____	cash deposit	_____
cash and carry	_____	cash disbursement	_____
cash balance	_____	cash discount	_____
cash bond	_____	cash dispenser	_____
cash credit	_____	cash dividend	_____

UNIT 30

INVESTMENT

Unsolicited investment advice is bad investment advice.

At this very minute, hundreds of "count executives" working for **brokerage houses** with fancy-sounding names you've never heard before are phoning prospective clients. Some are perfectly respectable – the modern equivalent of the clean-cut young men who used to work their way through college selling chrome-planted vacuum cleaners and leather – bound encyclopedias that no one really needed. Some are crooks, looking for suckers to buy rare coins at 20 times their market value or stocks in companies that specialize in recovering platinum from moonbeams.

Don't event try to figure out who's which. When you hear that friendly, confident voice on the other end of the line, hang up.

The investment that did wonders for your buddy Harry in the comptroller's office won't necessarily work for you.

No investment is perfect for everyone. The go-go mutual fund that makes sense for a happy –go-lucky bachelor with a good job could be pure poison for a couple approaching retirement with only Social Security and a small nest egg to fall back on. The municipal bond that doubles the after-tax return for a successful neurosurgeon in Boston could be a costly mistake for a schoolteacher in low –tax Florida.

Let Harry figure out what's best for Harry. Match your investments to your own tax situation, your ability to bear losses, and your need for read access to the cash.

When in doubt, diversify, diversify, diversify.

Some people think that the smartest investors in 1955 were the ones who put their entire life saving in a little – known company called Polaroid. But they weren't the smartest, just the luckiest. With hindsight, it is always easy to figure the best **investment strategy**. The trick is figuring it out before the fact . And for most people, most of the time it pays to divide money among a variety of investments.

There's more to diversification than the homily about not putting all your eggs in one basket. For one thing, merely mixing investments may not help to reduce risk: Buying $5.000 worth of five separate mutual funds that invest in **government bonds** may be no better than putting the whole $25.000 in a single mutual fund because all government bond funds tend to go up and down together with changes in interest rates.

Economists have something subtler – indeed, almost magical – in mind when they speak of the advantages of true diversification.

Helpful vocabulary:

account executive	المدير التنفيذي للحسابات
brokerage houses	بيوت السَّمْسَره
prospective clients	العملاء المحتملون
looking for suckers	يبحثون عن مغفلين
market value	القيمة السُّوقية ، سعر السُّوق
couple approaching retirement	زوجان على وشك التقاعد
costly mistake	خطأ جسيم
neurosurgeon	جَرَّاح أعصاب
tax situation	الوضع الضريبي
access to the cash	الوصول إلى النقد
smartest investors	أذكى المستثمرون
entire life savings	مُدَّخرات العُمْر
with hindsight	بالنظر الى الوراء
putting all your eggs in one basket	وضع البيض كله في سلة واحدة
to reduce risk	يقلِّل المخاطره
government bond	سندات حكومية
changes in interest rates	تغييرات في معدلات الفائدة
true diversification	تنويع حقيقي
risk of loss	مخاطرة الخسارة
expected return	العائد المتوقَّع
foreign stocks	أسهم أجنبية
business schools	كلية إدارة الأعمال
investment company	شركة إستثمار
mixed portfolio	محفظة مختلَطة

Exercise 1. *Translate the previous passage into Arabic.*

Exercise 2. *Fill in this table with the suitable English derivatives whenever possible, and write down the Arabic equivalents of all the words.*

	Verb		Noun		Adjective	
English	Arabic	English	Arabic	English	Arabic
		fancy			
need					
				confident	
		voice			
				friendly	
double					
				successful	
		tax			
		access			
				smart	
		strategy			
save					
match					
		average			
		energy			
speak					
		example			

Exercise 3. *Translate these terms:*

cash in advance	_____	cash payments	_____
cash market	_____	cash purchase	_____
cash on delivery	_____	cash received	_____
COD	_____	cash sale	_____
cash on receipt	_____	cash surplus	_____

135

UNIT 31

COMMERCIAL BANKS

COMMERCIAL banks are organized on a joint stock company system, primarily for the purpose of earning a profit. They can be either of the branch banking type, as we see in most of the countries, with a large network of branches, or of the unit banking type, as we see in the United States, where a bank's operations are confined to a single office or to a few branches within a strictly limited area. Although the **commercial banks** attract deposits of all kinds __ Current, Savings, and Fixed, their resources are chiefly drawn from current deposits, which are repayable on demand. So they attach much importance to the liquidity of their investments, and as such they specialize in satisfying the short –term credit needs of business other than the long-term.

The two essential functions of commercial banks may best be summarized as the borrowing and lending of money. They borrow money by taking all kinds of deposits. Deposits may be received on current account whereby the banker incurs the obligation of paying legal tender on demand, or on fixed deposit account whereby the banker incurs the obligation of paying legal tender after the expiry of a fixed period, or on **deposit account** whereby the banker undertakes to pay the customer an agreed rate of interest on it in return for the right to demand from him an agreed period of notice for withdrawals. Thus, a commercial banker, whether it be through **current account** or fixed deposit account, mobilizes the savings of the society. Then he provides this money to those who are in need of it by granting overdrafts or fixed loans or by discounting bills of exchange or promissory notes.

Thus, the primary function of a commercial banker is that of a broker and a dealer in money. By discharging this function efficiently, a **commercial banker** renders very valuable service to the community by increasing the productive capacity of the country and thereby accelerating the pace of economic development. He gathers the small savings of the people, thus reducing to the lowest limits idle money. Then he combines these small holdings in amounts large enough to be profitably employed those enterprises where they are most called for and most needed. Here, he makes capital effective and gives industry the benefits of capital, both of which otherwise would have remained idle. Take, for instance, the practice of discounting bills. By converting future claims into present money, the commercial banker bridges the time element between the sale and the actual payment of money. This will enable the seller to carry on his business without any hindrance, and the buyer will get enough time to realize the money.

Helpful vocabulary:

commercial bank	مصرِف تجاري
stock company	شركة مساهمة
network of branches	شبكة فروع
bank's operations	عمليات المصرِف
current deposits	ودائع جارية
fixed deposits	ودائع مربوطة لأجل
Savings deposits	ودائع مدخرات
repayable on demand	تدفع عند الطلب
short-term credit	تسليف قصير الأجل
borrowing and lending	استقراض وإقراض
current account	حسابٌ جارٍ
agreed rate of interest	نسبة فائدة متفق عليها
notice for withdrawals	إشعار بالسحوبات
expiry of a fixed period	انتهاء مدة محددة
in return for	مقابل
promissory notes	كمبيالات
pace of economic development	سرعة النمو الاقتصادي
idle money	أموال مُعَطَّلة
investment services	خدمات استثمارية
bank account	حساب مصرِفي
orders for purchase	طلبات الشراءِ
to fall due	يستحق
on behalf of	نيابة عن
share certificate	شهادة الأسهم

Exercise 1. *Translate the previous passage into Arabic.*

Exercise 2. *Fill in this table with the suitable English derivatives whenever possible, and write down the Arabic equivalents of all the words.*

Verb		Noun		Adjective	
English	Arabic	English	Arabic	English	Arabic
join					
organize					
		branch			
				commercial	
specialize					
		need			
save					
		deposit			
				valuable	
receive					
		service			
				profitable	
fix					
		subscription		new	
agree					
mobilize					
		group			

Exercise 3. *Translate these terms:*

certificate of deposit   ——————   certificate of registry   ——————

certificate of damage   ——————   certificate of stock   ——————

certificate of indebtedness   ——————   certificate check   ——————

certificate of insurance   ——————   chain stores   ——————

certificate of origin   ——————   charge sale   ——————

UNIT 32

DEPOSIT CONTRACTS AND
BANKING

In this chapter, a model of a bank is presented which focuses on the liquidity aspect of the banking business. We will show that there are efficiency gains from investing liquid funds into long-term illiquid assets. However, deposit banking which achieves these efficiency gains is vulnerable to bank runs. Furthermore, uncertainty about a bank's **investment projects** and adverse information may trigger a bank run. Before turning to these issues, however, we need briefly to discuss the role of money in an economy.

The theory of financial markets developed in the previous chapters leaves no room for financial institutions like banks that one observes in all modern economies. If trade in goods and assets is carried out only after all prices have been determined such that the **value of purchases** equals the value of sale, then there is no need for settlement of net trading positions. The market equilibria studied in the first part of this book were *frictionless* in this sense. In real economies, trade takes place sequentially, and buyers and sellers cannot expect to exchange goods and assets such that the **value of sales** equals the value or purchases for any two traders. Hence, usually, accredit relationship will arise between buyers and sellers in the course of any exchange. If trade took place only after equilibrium prices in all markets had been established, this would not matter since traders could be certain that the values of purchases and sales among all market participants would balance.

In actual economies, trade of goods and assets is not pre-co-ordinated by a general equilibrium **price system**. Hence, buyers and sellers must accept net credit positions based on trust that the trading partner will and can honor the obligation or they will have to settle the credit position by accepting some *means of payment*, that is *money*. In reality, exchanges of goods and assets are, therefore, usually accompanied by transfers of *money*. In the past, money was usually a good like gold which was easily storable and widely accepted in exchange. In modern economies, assets or portfolios of assets may serve the same purpose.

Money has value in exchange because it has a fairly stable price relative to the most commonly **traded goods**. It allows people to trade with each other who do not have goods or assets that they mutually desire.

Helpful vocabulary:

deposit contracts	عقود الودائع
banking business	الاعمال المصرفية
efficiency gains	مكاسب في الكفاءَة
liquid funds	أموال سائلة
long-term illiquid assets	أصول غير سائلة طويلة الأمد
bank run	سحب غير عادي للودائع
to leave no room for	لا يترك مجالاً لِ
such that	بِحَيثُ أنَّ
value of purchases	قيمة المشتريات
value of sales	قيمة المبيعات
trade of goods and assets	تجارة السِّلع والأصول
to honor the obligation	يحترم الالتزام
stable price	سِعْر مستقرّ
in compensation for a sale	عِوَضاً عن مبيعات
on the depositor's instruction	حساب تعليمات المودع
medium of exchange	وسيلة تبادل
to achieve a return	يحقق عائدا
payment system	نظام الدفع
prediction of withdrawals	التنبؤ بالسحوبات
deposit-taking	أخْذ الودائع
to pay on demand	يدَفْع عند الطلب
deposited money	النقود المودَعة

Exercise 1. *Translate the previous passage into Arabic.*

Exercise 2. *Fill in this table with the suitable English derivatives whenever possible, and write down the Arabic equivalents of all the words.*

	Verb		Noun		Adjective	
English	**Arabic**	**English**	**Arabic**	**English**	**Arabic**
present					
		efficiency			
				vulnerable	
focus					
invest					
		purchase			
				certain	
gain					
run					
achieve					
buy					
sell					
		trade			
equal					
		prediction			
exchange					
		excess			

Exercise 3. *Translate these terms:*

date of dispatch	_____	debit advice	_____
date of effect	_____	debit balance	_____
date of issue	_____	debit interest	_____
data of maturity	_____	debt management	_____
debit account	_____	debtor country	_____

UNIT 33

OVERVIEW OF FINANCIAL MARKETS

The main participants in financial market transactions are households, businesses (including financial institutions), and governments that purchase or sell financial assets. Those participants that provide funds are called **surplus units**, while participants that enter financial markets to obtain funds are called **deficit units**. The federal government commonly acts as a deficit unit. The Treasury finances the budget deficit by issuing Treasury securities. This main provider of funds are households and businesses. Foreign investors also commonly invest in U.S Treasury securities, as does the Federal Reserve System (the Fed). The Fed plays a major role in the financial markets because it controls the U.S. money supply and participates in the regulation of depository institutions.

Many participants in the **financial markets** simultaneously act as surplus and deficit units. For example, a business may sell new securities and use some of the proceeds to establish a checking account. Thus, funds are obtained from one type of financial market and used in another.

Primary Versus Secondary Markets

New securities are issued in primary markets, while exitsting securities are resold in secondary markets. primary **market transactions** provide funds to the initial issuer of securities; secondary market transactions do not. Some securities have a more active secondary market and are, therefore, more marketable than others. This is an important feature for financial market participants to know about if they plan to sell their security holdings prior to maturity. The issuance of new corporate stock or new Treasury securities represents a primary market transaction, while the sale of existing corporate stock or Treasury security holdings by any businesses or individuals represent a secondary market transaction.

Money Versus Capital Markets

Financial markets that facilitate the flow of short-term funds (with maturities less than one year) are known as **money markets**, while those that facilitate the flow of long-term funds are known as **capital markets**. Securities with a maturity of one year or less are called **money market securities**, whereas securities with maturity of more than one year are called **capital market securities**. Common stocks are classified as **capital market securities**, since they have no defined maturity. Money market securities generally have a higher degree of liquidity (can be liquidated easily without a loss of value).

Helpful vocabulary:

financial market transactions	معاملات السوق المالي
surplus units	وحدات الفائض
deficit unit	وحدات العجز
federal government	الحكومة الاتحادية
budget deficit	عجز الميزانية
Federal Reserve System	نظام الاحتياطي الاتحادي
checking account	حسابٌ جارٍ
more marketable	أكثر قابلية للتسويق
prior to maturity	قبل الاستحقاق
money market	سوق العملة
capital market	سوق رأس المال
degree of liquidity	درجة السيولة
annualized return	عائد سنوي
New York Stock Exchange	السوق المالي في نيويورك
OTC market	سوق خارج السوق الرسمية
in response to demand	استجابة للطلب
tax status	الوضع الضريبي
individual investor	مستثمر فردي
institutional investor	مستثمر مؤسسي
bond prices	أسعار السندات
market response	استجابة السوق
market participants	المشتركون في السوق

Exercise 1. *Translate the previous passage into Arabic.*

Exercise 2. *Fill in this table with the suitable English derivatives whenever possible, and write down the Arabic equivalents of all the words.*

	Verb		Noun		Adjective
English	Arabic	English	Arabic	English	Arabic
purchase					
		participant			
sell					
provide					
		fund			
invest					
		regulation			
use					
proceed					
		liquid			
represent					
				preferable	
plan					
		instrument			
				immediate	
issue					
		position			
return					

Exercise 3. *Translate these terms:*

easy terms	——————	eligible investment	————
economic statistics	——————	employee motivation	————
economic stability	——————	employee morale	————
economic self-sufficiency	——————	employee office	————
elastic currency	——————	employee volume	————

147

UNIT 34

THE IMPORTANCE OF LEMDING

The aim of this chapter is to introduce commercial lending and in particular consider the context and environment in which the lending decision is made. In recent times, **commercial lending** has seen some dramatic changes. Although the main clearing banks still tend to dominate the commercial lending market, this stranglehold is in decline. Other institutions have entered the market, for example, foreign banks and building societies, which are vigorously active in pushing up their own market share. Differing **sources of finance** have also emerged as important contributors to commercial funding, such as leasing. Government has also tended to be more pro-active and interventionist in the commercial lending market. At the same time, the commercial lending institutions have themselves gone through dramatic changes in terms of banking philosophy, the products marketed, and the introduction of new technology. All these changes in commercial lending and its environment will be influential on the way in which banks make lending decisions and the way in which they operate.

This chapter begins by briefly examining bank lending in relation to other sources of business finance. A discussion follows relating to bankers' assessment of risk. Finally, a brief summary is provided of the scope and structure of the book.

In examining bank lending in relation to other sources of finance, we will consider the extent to which bank lending is used compared to other sources of commercial finance and how these sources are generally utilized by **commercial borrowers**. Unfortunately, we cannot be precise as to the extent of bank lending *vis-à-vis* other sources of finance because there are no readily a available statistics. However, we can look at some of the evidence regarding these sources and make some observations relating to the use of these sources of finance by business. Through this analysis, we will be in a better position to understand the role of commercial bank lending in relation to the firm and its contribution to the economy as a whole.

In **finance theory**, it is the convention to categorize sources of finance into long term, medium term, and short term. The needs of business differ over these time horizons and, not surprisingly, the nature of the funding to support the business activity will also differ in character. Although it is not appropriate here so list and describe all the many types of long, medium, or short-term finance, reference will be made to the main types. More detailed information regarding the various types of finance can be found in general finance texts.

Helpful vocabulary:

commercial lending	إقراض تجاري
lending decision	قرار الإقراض
clearing banks	مَصْرِف مُقَاصَّة
in decline	في تراجع ، في هبوط
its market share	حصتها في السوق
commercial funding	تمويل تجاري
products markets	أسواق المنتوجات
bank lending	إقراض مصرفي
assessment of risk	تقييم المخاطرة
commercial borrowers	مقترضون تجاريون
as to the extent	في ما يتعلق بمدى
available statistics	إحصائيات جاهزة
to be in a better position to	يكون في وضع أفضل لـ
finance theory	نظرية التمويل
long –term finance	تمويل بعيد الأمد
medium –term finance	تمويل متوسط الأمد
short-term finance	تمويل قصير الأمد
repayment date	تاريخ التسديد
equity holders	حاملو الأسهم
bank loan	قرض مصرفي
convertible loan	قرض قابل للتحويل
debt finance	تمويل بالاقتراض
with the exception of	باستثناء
working capital	رأسمالُ العاملُ
to be sourced from	يَرِد مِنْ

Exercise 1. *Translate the previous passage into Arabic.*

Exercise 2. *Fill in this table with the suitable English derivatives whenever possible, and write down the Arabic equivalents of all the words.*

	Verb		Noun		Adjective
English	**Arabic**	**English**	**Arabic**	**English**	**Arabic**
relate					
				vigorous	
follow					
		summary			
				brief	
lend					
		structure			
borrow					
		example			
provide					
		commerce			
decide					
		finance			
make					
		drama			
		fund			
push					

Exercise 3. *Translate these terms:*

face value	_____	filing system	_____
factoring company	_____	finance company	_____
factory price	_____	financial ledger	_____
false money	_____	fire insurance	_____
false check	_____	fixed premium	_____

UNIT 35

THE ACCOUNTS OF A
TRADING CONCERN

A trading concern is one which earns its profits from the activates of buying and selling; by purchasing items at one price and selling them at a higher price, the firm seeks to generate its income. This buying and selling activity is known as *trading*.

Trading is an important activity. It is people involved in trade who bring to us many of the items which we consume each day. The *retail trade* in Britain employs over 2 million people. It is spread over nearly 400.000 outlets, operated by over a quarter of a million businesses. These businesses are responsible for a turnover in excess of £40,000 million each year.

Throughout the whole of this **trading activity**, money flows into, through, and out of the businesses. Money from customers flows in from the goods and services sold by the firms; and money flows out to pay the firms' own suppliers.

In order to keep a record of these flows of money, each individual business needs to operate some form of accounting system, such as is illustrated below.

Prime documents are such records as invoices received from supplies, copies of invoices sent to customers, cheque stubs, gas bills etc. Although some of these will flow into the business from suppliers of goods and services, others will be produced by the firm itself. These prime documents will be processed into the principal book of account, which is the **ledger**.

Within the ledger itself, the financial records are kept in **accounts**, each account being devoted to transactions of a particular kind or concerning particular people. The ledger may, thus, contain an account for fuel and power, and a separate one for rent and rates. Each debtor will have a separate account: so, too, will each creditor.

It is likely that these accounts will be kept on the conventional double *entry system*, whereby the account is divided vertically into two parts: the **debit** side and the **credit** side. Each transaction will be entered once on the debit (left) side of an account, and once on the credit (right) side of another account. It is this practice of entering transactions twice which gives rise to the term 'double entry' bookkeeping. Increasingly, however, a vertical format is now used.

Helpful vocabulary:

trading concern	مصلحة تجارية
trading	متاجرة، تجارة
retail trade	تجارة التجزئة
turnover in excess of	تداول بما يزيد عن
Dept of Trade	وزارة التجارة
prime documents	الوثائق الأساسية
invoices from suppliers	فواتير من المُورِّدين
cheque stab	كَعْب الشيك
ledger	دفتر الأستاذ
fuel and power	البنزين والكهرباء ، الوقود والطاقة
debtor and creditor	مدين ودائن
separate account	حساب منفصل
double entry system	طريقة القيد المزدوج
increases in assets	زيادات في الأصولِ
accounting record	سجل محاسبي
credit balance	رصيد دائن
debit balance	رصيد مدين
credit entries	قيودات دائنة
debit entries	قيودات مدينة
bought ledger	دفتر الأستاذ للمشتريات
sales ledger	دفتر الأستاذ للمبيعات
nominal ledger	دفتر الأستاذ الاسميّ

Exercise 1. *Translate the previous passage into Arabic.*

Exercise 2. *Fill in this table with the suitable English derivatives whenever possible, and write down the Arabic equivalents of all the words.*

	Verb		Noun		Adjective
English	Arabic	English	Arabic	English	Arabic
		trade			
generate					
		excess			
employ					
purchase					
		form			
flow					
		record			
operate					
illustrate					
		service			
supply					
		loss			
pay					
		debit			
receive					
		credit			

Exercise 3. *Translate these terms:*

general expenses	_____	goods in stock	_____
general tariff	_____	government revenues	_____
general manager	_____	green goods	_____
goods returned	_____	gross earnings	_____
goods in bulk	_____	gross sales	_____

UNIT 36

FINANCIAL STATEMENTS

The three major financial statements include the balance sheet, the income statement, and the statement of cash flows. These statements are prepared at the end of the **accounting period** and are based on generally accepted accounting principles.

The *balance sheet*, illustrated in Figure 1.1, reflects assets and claims to assets of the hypothetical Mayfair Hotel. Assets simply are items of value to the hotel company. The first claims to assets are by the creditors, and these claims are referred to as *liabilities*. The claims which must be paid within a relatively short period of time are labelled as *current liabilities*, while other obligations of the hotel company at the balance sheet date are *long-term liabilities*. The residual claims to assets are by the owners and are revealed in the owners' equity section of the balance sheet. The claims to assets equal the assets; thus, this is the reason why this financial statement is called the **balance sheet**.

Assets are classified as current assets, investments, and property and equipment, as shown in Figure 1.1. The balance sheet is a static statement as it is prepared as of a given date, the last day of the accounting period. This statement reflects the *accounting equation* of assets equal liabilities plus owners' equity. The balance sheet of the Mayfair Hotel reveals assets of $1,176,300 and liabilities and owners' equity for the same amount on December 31.19x2.

The financial statement which reflects operations of the Mayfair Hotel is the *income statement*, as illustrated in Figure 1.2. The income statement includes both **revenues** (sales) and **expenses**. The income statement illustrated in this chapter contains considerable detail and reflects activity by areas of responsibility. The top section of the income statement contains the revenue, payroll and related costs, other direct expenses, and departmental income of $605,000 for 19x2. The second section reflects the operations of the food and beverage department.

Balance sheets

Mayfair Hotel

December 31,19x0, 19x1, 19x2

Assets 19x0 19x1 19x2

Current assets:

	19x0	19x1	19x2
Cash	$17.000	$ 18.000	$21.000
Marketable securities	81.000	81.000	81.000
Account receivable (net)	100.000	90.000	140.000
Inventories	17.000	20.000	18.000
Prepaid expenses	13.000	12.000	14.000
Total current assets	228.000	221.000	274.000

Helpful vocabulary:

financial statement	بيان مالي
balance sheet	ميزانية عامة
income statement	بيان الدخلِ
accounting period	فترة محاسبية
cash flows	حركة النقد
hotel company	شركة فندقية
current liabilities	ديون حالية ، التزامات قصيرة الأجل
long –term liabilities	ديون بعيدة الأجل
given date	تاريخ محدد
owners' equity	حقوق المالكين
accounting equation	المعادلة المحاسبية
revenues and expenses	الإيرادات والمصروفات
marketable securities	أوراق مالية قابلة للتسويق
accounts receivable	حساب مدين
prepaid expenses	مصروفات مدفوعة مقدماً
total current assets	إجمالي الأصول الحالية
accumulated depreciation	هبوط القيمة التراكمي
accrued income taxes	ضرائب الدخل المتجمعة
deferred income taxes	ضرائب الدخل المُؤَجلة
retained earnings	أرباح محتجزة

Exercise 1. *Translate the previous passage into Arabic.*

Exercise 2. *Fill in this table with the suitable English derivatives whenever possible, and write down the Arabic equivalents of all the words.*

	Verb		Noun		Adjective
English	Arabic	English	Arabic	English	Arabic
state					
		finance			
prepare					
		balance			
				general	
		end			
accept					
		period			
reflect					
		value			
claim					
		date			
oblige					
		residue			

Exercise 3. *Translate these terms:*

hard currency	———————	housing corporation	———————
health insurance	———————	hush money	———————
heavy loss	———————	illegal sale	———————
home market	———————	import deposit	———————
home consumption	———————	immediate shipment	———————

UNIT 37

THE FRAMEWORK FOR ACCOUNTING AND FINANCIAL PERORTING
FOR GOVERNMENTAL
AND NOT-FOR-PROFIT
ORGANAIZATIONS

Many persons who practice accounting and many who teach accounting maintain that there is only one " body of generally accepted accounting principle" (GAAP) which applies to accounting and financial reporting by all entities. Although a number of attempts have been made, no one has ever succeeded in producing a definitive description of universal GAAP. In place of a concise statement of GAAP, a series *of statements of accounting* and financial reporting standards have been issued by organizations whose pronouncements are accepted as authoritative. One such organization in the United States is the Financial Accounting Standards Board (FASB). The FASB sets standards for financial reports published by profit – seeking businesses for distribution to **stockholders**, creditors, and others not actively involved in the management of the business.

A second organization, the Governmental Accounting Standards

Board (GASB), has been established to set accounting and financial reporting standards for state and local governments in the United States. A separate standards – setting organization was considered necessary because governments have no stockholders or other owners, they render service with no expectation of earning **net income**, and they have the power to require taxpayers to support financial operation whether or not they receive benefits in proportion to taxes paid. Further, the form of government in the United States requires interrelationships between a state government and local governments established in conformity with state law, and interrelationships within any one government between the executive and legislative branches, which have no parallel in business organizations. Thus, it is to be expected that GASB standards, discussed in the chapters of this book devoted to accounting for state and local governments, differ in many respects from FASB standards discussed in book concerned with **financial accounting** for businesses.

Commonly , colleges and universities , hospitals , voluntary health and welfare organizations, libraries, museums, churches, and so on are similar to governments in that they exist to render service to constituents with no expectation of earning net income from those services, have no owners, and seek *financial resources* from persons who do not expect either repayment or **economic benefits** proportionate to the resources provided.

Helpful vocabulary:

definitive description	وصف محدّد ، وصف تعريفي
in place of	بدلاً من
financial reporting standards	معايير التقرير المالي
FASB	مجلس معايير المحاسبة المالية
GASB	مجلس معايير المحاسبة الحكومية
GAAP	مبادئ المحاسبة المقبولة عامةً
profit –seeking businesses	شركات باحثة عن الربح
to render service	يقدم خدمات
standards- setting organization	منظمةً محددة للمعايير
in proportion to	متناسبة مع
state law	قانون الولاية
in conformity with	متماشياً مع، منسجماً مع
no parallel	لا نظير لها
in many respects	في جوانب عديدة
similar ... in that	مشابهة ... من حيث
economic benefits	عوائد اقتصادية
nongovernmental entity	مؤسسة غير حكومية
not –for –profit entity	مؤسسة غير ربحية
AICPA	المعهد الأمريكي للمحاسبين العامين المجازين
conceptual considerations	اعتبارات مفاهيمية
body of standards	مجموعة معايير
to address broad issues	يعالج مشكلات واسعة

Exercise 1. *Translate the previous passage into Arabic.*

Exercise 2. *Fill in this table with the suitable English derivatives whenever possible, and write down the Arabic equivalents of all the words.*

	Verb		Noun		Adjective
English	Arabic	English	Arabic	English	Arabic
practice					
maintain					
				concise	
accept					
succeed					
				local	
seek					
involve					
		authority			
				separate	
hold					
		profit			
own					
				broad	
render					
		standard			
require					

Exercise 3. *Translate these terms:*

installment bond	_____	intermediate goods	_____
installment loan	_____	internal auditor	_____
insurable property	_____	interim receipt	_____
insurance broker	_____	interim accounts	_____
insurance register	_____	interest rates	_____

UNIT 38

OBJECTIVES AND ENVIRONMENT
OF ACCOUNTING

Accounting can be defined as the collection and processing (analysis, measurement, and recording) of financial data about an organization and the reporting of that information to decision makers. An **accounting system** processes data concerning the (a) flows of resources into and out of an organization, (b) resources controlled (i.e., assets) by the organization, and (c) claims against those resources (i.e., debts). The flow of accounting information is summarized in Exhibit 1__1. Notice that the end products of an accounting system are **financial statements** that are prepared for decision makers.

Economics has a special relationship with accounting. Economics is the study of how people and society choose to employ scarce productive resources that could have alternative uses to produce various commodities and distribute them for consumption, now or in the future, among various persons and group in society. Like economics, accounting has a conceptual foundation of financial information about an organization. In general, accounting reports how an entity has allocated its scarce resources. Thus, accounting collects, measures, interprets, and reports **financial information** on the same activities that are the focus of economics. Economics explains economic relationships on a conceptual level, whereas accounting reports the economic relationships primarily on a practical level. However, accounting measurements are as consistent with economic concepts as is possible. Accounting must cope with the complex and practical problems of measuring in monetary terms the economic effects of **exchange transactions** (i.e., resource inflows and outflows). These effects relate to the resources held and the claims against the resources of an entity. Throughout this textbook, the theoretical and practical issues that arise in the measurement process are discussed from the accounting viewpoint.

The *environment* in which accounting operates is effected by such forces as the type of (*a*) government (e.g., democracy versus communism), (*c*) industry (e.g., technological versus agrarian), (*d*) organizations within that society (e.g., labor unions), and (e) regulatory controls (i.e., private sector versus governmental). Accounting is influenced significantly by the educational level and economic development of the society.

Helpful vocabulary:

reporting of information	إبلاغ المعلومات
decision makers	صُنّاع القرار
flow of accounting information	تدفُّق المعلومات المحاسبية
communication of financial information	نقل المعلومات المالية
conceptual level	المستوى النظري ، المستوى المفهومي
from the accounting viewpoint	مِنْ وجهة نظر محاسبية
evolving needs of the society	الحاجات المتطورة للمجتمع
diverse and complex	متنوع و معقّد
significant inflation	تضّخم كبير ، تضخمُّ هام
sole proprietorship	مِلكية فردية
partnership contract	عقد شراكة تضامنية
division of income	تقاسُم الدخلِ
reporting period	فترة الإبلاغ
distribution of resources	توزيع الموارد
alternative uses	أستخدامات بديلة
free enterprise	نشاط اقتصادي حر
governmental sector	القطاع الحكومي
sound decisions	قرارات سليمة
in direct proportion to	بنسبة طردية مع ، بنسبة مباشرة مع
to meet this need	ليلبِّي هذه الحاجة
unique environment	البيئة الفريدة

166

Exercise 1. *Translate the previous passage into Arabic.*

Exercise 2. *Fill in this table with the suitable English derivatives whenever possible, and write down the Arabic equivalents of all the words.*

	Verb		Noun		Adjective	
English	Arabic	English	Arabic	English	Arabic
measure					
		capital			
define					
		retail			
discuss					
				separate	
		contract			
educate					
				legal	
strengthen					
		exchange			
				allocated	
follow					
		effect			
				theoretical	
				scarce	

Exercise 3. *Translate these terms:*

job announcement	———————	joint agreement	———————
job evaluation	———————	joint committee	———————
job description	———————	joint creditor	———————
job costing	———————	joint debtor	———————
joint account	———————	joint endorsement	———————

167

UNIT 39

WHOMEN IN MANAGEMENT

Women occupy only about 10 per cent of *management positions* in Europe. Furthermore, women managers remain concentrated in junior and middle **management positions**: very few have managed to break through the 'glass ceiling' to occupy the top jobs.

It is difficult to put a more accurate figure on the numbers of women in management in Europe, first because different countries may have a different definition of '*manager*', and secondly because in many countries there are no regularised systems of gathering statistics in this area. Davidson and Cooper (1993) estimate that women occupy fewer than 5 per cent of senior management roles, and suggest that this figure many be as high as 8 per cent in Greece and as low as 2 per cent in the United Kingdom. However, they estimate that, when all levels of management are considered, the United Kingdom has the highest number of women 'managers' at 26 per cent, compared with France at 25 per cent and Ireland at 17.4 per cent.

Even so, British industry is an overwhelmingly male bastion, dominated by middle _ aged men who play golf and who have been to public school and Oxbridge. Over the past two years, the number of *women managers* actually fell. The recession has pushed the equal opportunities timetable off the industrial agenda temporarily in those businesses struggling to survive. In the 1980s, women were going to fill the gap left by the demographic time bomb, by an anticipated drop of 25 per cent in the number of 18- year-olds and by skill shortages. The single European market also helped to create job opportunities for women. This situation has now altered, for the moment. With unemployment at around 3 million, the skill shortages issue is no longer the issue it once was, but it is still a concern even if the skill shortages are more segmented. For, example, the **banking industry**, which has been a major employer of women, is down-sizing and therefore, not experiencing a skill shortage at present. However, it would be a mistake to think that the demographic bomb has been defused. Instead of focusing on solving skill shortages, women are providing the flexibility, and new management styles are needed in business in the 1990s to enhance performance.

Figures gathered by Antal and Krebsbach-Gnath suggest that in the former West Germany 23.3 per cent of public sector managers are female, compared with only 5.9 per cent of private sector managers. Germany shows a high degree of **job segregation** by sex. In the former West Germany, for example, 70 per cent of women are concentrated in 10 occupational categories: Women account for 86 per cent of people employed in the health services, 79 per cent in the social services, 62 per cent in retailing, and 48 per cent in teaching.

Helpful vocabulary:

management positions	مواقع إدارية
women managers	المديرات
junior and middle positions	المواقع الصغرى والوسطى
top jobs	الوظائف العليا
gathering statistics	جمع الإحصاءات
middle-aged men	رجالٍ في وسط العُمْر
equal opportunities	الفرص المتكافئة
industrial agenda	جدول الأعمال الصناعي
demographic time bomb	القنبلة الموقوتة السكانية
anticipated drop	انخفاض متوقّع
skill shortages issue	مشكلة نقصان المهارات
for the moment	مؤقتاً
bank industry	الصناعة المصرفية
is down-sizing	تقلص حجمها
public-sector managers	مدراء القطاعِ العام
job segregation by sex	الفصل الوظيفي حسب الجنس
health services	خدمات صحية
cadre occupations	وظائف إدارية
chief executive	مدير تنفيذي
nursery school	مدرسة حضانة
part-time employment	توظيف بالدوام الجزئي
company directors	مدراء الشركات
less career-oriented in	أقل اهتماماً بالوظيفة
tend to be concentrated in	تميل الى التركُّز في

Exercise 1. *Translate the previous passage into Arabic.*

Exercise 2. *Fill in this table with the suitable English derivatives whenever possible, and write down the Arabic equivalents of all the words.*

Verb		Noun		Adjective	
English	**Arabic**	**English**	**Arabic**	**English**	**Arabic**
		position			
		number			
estimate					
		statistics			
gather					
		situation			
				regular	
unite					
		school			
				high	
employ					
		drop			
anticipate					
		segregation			
				particular	
concentrate					

Exercise 3. *Translate these terms:*

labor cost	———————	landed estate	———————
labor contract	———————	landing certificate	———————
labor law	———————	landing sale	———————
labor market	———————	landlord liability	———————
land bank	———————	lapsed coupon	———————

UNIT 40

PURPOSE OF ACCOUNTING

Accounting provides a record of *business transactions* in financial terms. Accounting records are needed by profit-making enterprises and by **nonprofit-making organizations**, such as governmental units, fiduciaries and associations operating for religious, philanthropic, or fraternal purposes. Records of the financial transactions of an individual or a family are considered a necessity at times.

In a business enterprise, *managerial decisions*, whether of great or small import to the activities of the business, must often rely on the **accounting records** for information to guide the firm on a profitable and solvent course. Thus, the primary purpose of accounting for any organization is to provide management with the information needed for its efficient operation. Accounting should also make available the financial information properly desired by governmental agencies, present and prospective creditors and investors, and the general public.

Bookkeeping is the systematic recording of business transactions in financial terms. Accounting covers a wider field, which includes bookkeeping and involves the design of **business records**, data analysis, preparation of reports based on the records, and interpretation of the reports. Usually, the study of bookkeeping emphasizes technique, whereas the study of accounting emphasizes theory.

The three major financial statements are: *the balance sheet*, the *income statement*, and the *statement of changes* in *financial position or funds statement*, the *balance sheet* (statement of financial position) provides a list of **assets**, liabilities, and proprietorship or capital of a business entity as of a specific date; the *income statement* (statement of operating results) summarizes the income and expenses of a business entity for a specific period of time; and the *funds statement* (statement of changes in financial position) indicates the source from which funds were acquired during the accounting period covered by the report and the disposition made of them.

A business transaction is an action that involves an exchange of values. It is the occurrence of an event or a condition that is financial in nature and should be recorded in terms of money. Purchases and sales of goods or services are examples. Accounting records show the effects of **business transactions** on the assets, liabilities, and proprietorship of a business.

Helpful vocabulary:

business transactions	معاملات تجارية
profit-making enterprises	مشاريع ربحية
non-profit organization	منظمات غير ربحية
managerial decisions	قرارات إدارية
accounting records	سجلات محاسبية
efficient operation	تشغيل كُفْء
governmental agencies	وكالات حكومية
present and prospective creditors	الدائنون الحاليون والمتوقعون
data analysis	تحليل البيانات
interpretation of reports	تفسير التقارير
financial statements	بيانات مالية
balance sheet	الميزانية العامة
income statement	بيان الدخل
funds statement	بيان الأموال
financial position	الوضع المالي
business entity	كيان تجاري
assets and liabilities	الاصول والديون ، الموجودات والالتزامات
subjective opinion	رأي ذاتي
values on the books	القيم في الدفاتر (المحاسبية)
current value	القيمة الحالية
amount of depreciation	كمية هبوط القيمة

Exercise 1. *Translate the previous passage into Arabic.*

Exercise 2. *Fill in this table with the suitable English derivatives whenever possible, and write down the Arabic equivalents of all the words.*

	Verb		Noun		Adjective
English	Arabic	English	Arabic	English	Arabic
provide					
need					
		profit			
				philanthropic	
		record			
				fraternal	
desire					
		necessity			
manage					
		import			
base					
		system			
				wide	
state					
		design			
fund					

Exercise 3. *Translate these terms:*

letter of advice	_____	letter of trust	_____
letter of credit	_____	life policy	_____
letter of delegation	_____	liquid funds	_____
letter of guarantee	_____	liquid ratio	_____
letter of introduction	_____	live storage	_____

UNIT 41

SOURCE AND METHODOLOGY OF
ACCOUNTING PRINCIPLES

Accounting records dating back several thousand years have
been found in various parts of the world. These records indicate
that at all levels of development people desire information about
their efforts and accomplishments. For example, the Zenon papyri,
which were discovered in 1915, contain information about the
construction projects, agricultural activities, and *business operations*
of the private estate of Apollonius for a period of about thirty years
during the third century B.C.

Accounting to Hain, "the Zenon papyri give evidence of a
surprisingly elaborate accounting system which had been used in
Greece since the fifth century B.C. and which, in the wake of Greek
trade or conquest, gradually spread throughout the Eastern
Mediterranean and Middle East." The accounting system used by
zenon contained provisions for responsibility accounting, a written
record of all transactions, a personal account for wages paid to
employees, **inventory records**, and a record of asset acquisitions
and disposals. In addition, there is evidence that all

of the accounts were audited.

Although the Zenon papyri and other records indicate that *accounting practice* has a long history, most organized efforts at developing *accounting theory* have occurred since 1930. Individual writes such as Sprague, Hatfield, Kester, and Paton made significant contributions before that time (in the early 1900s), but those contributions did not receive widespread acceptance and did not have the influence of the more organized efforts of recent years.

One of the first attempts at improving accounting began shortly after the Great Depression with a series of meetings between representatives of the New York Stock Exchange (NYSE) and the American Institute of Accountants (now American Institute of Certified public Accountant or AICPA). The purpose of these meetings was to discuss problems pertaining to the interests of **investors**, the NYSE, and accountants in the preparation of external finical statements.

Similarly, in 1935 the American Association of University Instructors in Accounting changed its name to the American Accounting Association (AAA) and announced its intention to expand its activities in the research and development of accounting principles and standards.

Helpful vocabulary:

accounting principles	مبادئ المحاسبة ، مبادئ محاسبية
construction projects	مشاريع إنشائية
business operations	عمليات تجارية
accounting system	نظام محاسبي
in the wake of	في بداية
Greek conquest	الغزو اليوناني
responsibility accounting	المحاسبة المسؤولة
audited accounts	حسابات مدققة
Great Depression	الكساد الكبير
N Y S E	السوق المالي في نيويورك
interests of investors	مصالح المستثمرين
A A A	جمعية المحاسبة الأمريكية
tentative statement	بيان مؤقت
so much remains	يبقى الكثير
theoretical basis	أساس نظري
practice of accounting	مهنة المحاسبة ، ممارسة المحاسبة
revision in wording	مراجعة الصياغة
to the effect that	مُفَاده أنَّ
in accordance with	طِبقَاً لِ
to comply with	يلتزم بـ
authoritative organizations	منظمات ذات نفوذ

Exercise 1. *Translate the previous passage into Arabic.*

Exercise 2. *Fill in this table with the suitable English derivatives whenever possible, and write down the Arabic equivalents of all the words.*

Verb		Noun		Adjective	
English	Arabic	English	Arabic	English	Arabic
		acquisition			
		acceptance			
				private	
indicate					
		influence			
				personal	
contain					
		surprise			
				gradual	
develop					
		Greece			
discover					
		period			
				coherent	
wake					
		theory			
compare					
		effect			

Exercise 3. *Translate these terms:*

maintenance costs	——	manufacturing overhead	——
management consultant	——	merchandise mark	——
management accounts	——	merchant marine	——
managing director	——	monetary reform	——
manufacturing accounting	——	monetary reserves	——

UNIT 42

A PARTNERSHIP AGREEMENT

The partnership Act 1890 stipulates that the following rules apply in the absence of an agreement to the contrary (note that the rules are not mandatory).

The interests of partners in the **partnership property**, and their rights and duties in relation to the partnership shall be determined, subject to any agreement, express or implied, between the partners by the following rules:

(1) All the partners are entitled to share equally in the capital and profits of the business, and must contribute equally towards the losses, whether of capital or otherwise, sustained by the firm.

(2) The firm must indemnify every partner in respect of payments made and **personal liabilities** incurred by him:

> (a) in the ordinary and proper conduct at the business of the firm ; or
>
> (b) in or about anything necessarily done for the preservation of the business or property of the firm.

(3) Whether the capitals are to be fixed, drawings and profits being adjusted on current accounts, or whether they are to be adjusted on the **capital accounts**.

(4) A partner is not entitled, before the ascertainment of profits, to interest on the capital subscribed by him.

(5) Every partner may take part in the management of the partnership business.

(6) No partner shall be entitled to remuneration for acting in the partnership business.

(7) No person may be introduced as a partner without the consent of all existing partners.

(8) any difference arising as to ordinary matters connected with the partnership business may be decided by a majority of the partners, but no change may by made in the nature of the partnership business without the consent of all existing partners.

(9) The **partnership books** are to be kept at the place of business of the partnership (or the principal place, if there is more than one), and every partner may , when he thinks fit, have access to and inspect and copy any of them.

Helpful vocabulary:

partnership act	اتفاقية شركة التضامن
partnership act	قانون شركات التضامن
agreement to the contrary	اتفاقية تنص على خلاف ذلك
interests of partners	مصالح الشركاءِ
express or implied	صراحة أو ضمناً
to be entitled to	يستحق
capital and profits	رأس المال والأرباح
in respect of	فيما يتعلق بِ
current account	حسابٌ جارٍ
capital account	حساب رأس المال
existing partners	الشركاء الحاليون
partners' drawings	مسحوبات الشركاءِ
fixed capital	رأس المال الثابت
undrawn profits	أرباح غير مسحوبة
in excess of	زيادة عن ، تجاوزاً لِ
loan account	حساب القروض
repayable on dissolution	مستحق للتسديد عند التصفية
5% per annum	5 % سنوياً
under the Act	بموجب القانون
profit and loss account	حساب الارباح والخسائر
net profit	صافي الأرباح
interest on capital	الفائدة على رأس المال

Exercise 1. *Translate the previous passage into Arabic.*

Exercise 2. *Fill in this table with the suitable English derivatives whenever possible, and write down the Arabic equivalents of all the words.*

	Verb		Noun		Adjective
English	Arabic	English	Arabic	English	Arabic
stipulate					
		absence			
				contrary	
determine					
express					
		rule			
imply					
entitle					
		loss			
sustain					
contribute					
		preservation			
		consent			
inspect					
		change			
draw					
		danger			

Exercise 3. Translate these terms:

net asset ——————— net pay ———————

net costs ——————— net price ———————

net balance ——————— net profit ———————

net loss ——————— net return ———————

net income ——————— net sales ———————

UNIT 43

MANAGER –EMPLOYEE
RELATIONS

For three hundred years, there was a widespread totalitarian attitude on the part of supervisors: "'Do it my way or you're fired." Since the *1960s* , *manager-employee relations* have changed considerably and continue to change at a rapid rate. In today's workplace, there are certain employee rights and freedoms supported to a great extent by state and federal laws as well as by special interest groups. These rights and freedoms cannot be sidestepped by the supervisor. They must be understood, seriously considered, an intelligently implemented.

The supervisor - the manager having the closest contact with the workers - is the individual most frequently confronted with the problem of dealing with changing attitudes of employees. The most likely area of confrontation is in alleged discrimination, where an employee feels that he or she is not being given fair consideration. When these attitudinal situations occur, they must quickly resolved, often by the first-level supervisor, to avoid their becoming agitations that spread to other employees and / or involve outside special interest groups. It is a real challenge to resolve attitudinal problems because the facts are so often "fuzzy" and the individuals involved are usually very emotional about the situation.

Another employee area undergoing significant change is labor union-management relations. Inflation with its resulting *cost escalation*, foreign competition, rising energy costs, greater demands for quality control, and decreasing worker productivity are bringing about attitudinal changes on the part of both labor leaders and managers. The labor relations pendulum over a period of time has swung from the side of management to that of **labor unions**. There are now many indicators that the gap between labor and management is closing. Participative management between the two groups appears to be more prevalent, with both sides making significant concessions.

A third factor affecting manager-employee relations is the changing composition of the *work force*. Women, older workers, and handicapped persons are becoming more common in jobs once thought to be inappropriate for them. Some are accepted by their peers, and some are not. It is a challenge for the supervisor to effectively integrate these groups of workers into a unified work force.

A major challenge for today's supervisors is to develop a more paternalistic and participative approach to management problem solving and decision making. In this area of management there is much to be learned from the Japanese concept of **quality control** circles.

185

Helpful vocabulary:

totalitarian attitude	موقف استبدادي
manager -employee relations	العلاقات بين المدير والموظفين
employee rights	حقوق الموظفين
intelligently implemented	تُطبَّق بذكاء
closest contract	الاتصال الأوثق
is confronted with	يواجَهُ بِ
alleged discrimination	التمييز المزعوم
labor union	اتحاد العمالِ
resulting cost escalation	تصاعد التكاليف الناجم
labor union	اتحاد العمالِ
resulting cost escalation	تصاعد التكاليف الناجم
rising energy costs	تكاليف الطاقة المتزايدة
quality control	ضبط الجودة ، ضبط النوعية
decreasing worker productivity	إنتاجية العامل المتناقصة
labor leaders	زعماء العمال ، قادة العمال
participative management	إدارة مشتركة
significant concessions	تنازلات هامة
work force	القوة العاملة
the common good	الصالح العام
managerial responsibility	مسؤولية إدارية
job assignments	واجبات الوظيفية
decision making	صنع القرار
to solve problems	يحَلّ المشاكلِ

Exercise 1. *Translate the previous passage into Arabic.*

Exercise 2. *Fill in this table with the suitable English derivatives whenever possible, and write down the Arabic equivalents of all the words.*

Verb		Noun		Adjective	
English	Arabic	English	Arabic	English	Arabic
		escalation			
				significant	
		competition			
				attitudinal	
		indicator			
				prevalent	
		concession			
				participative	
		parent			
				individual	
assign					
		profit			
				flexible	
limit					
				Japanese	
implement					
cooperate					

Exercise 3. *Translate these terms:*

on board	_____	open credit	_____
on account	_____	opening price	_____
on order	_____	open market	_____
open bid	_____	open policy	_____
open check	_____	open trade	_____

UNIT 44

ACCOUNTING AS A CAREER

Some accountants also earn the Public American (CPA) designation. Each state sets standards that persons must meet to earn the CPA. These standards usually include passing a rigorous examination and having a specified amount of accounting experience. In some states, college accounting study can be substituted for some of there required experience. The CPA designation is important to *professional accountants*. The public knows that CPA's are accounting professionals. Public accounting firms often require that accounting employees earn CPA to be eligible for promotion to top position. Many businesses also require that top accounting persons earn the CAP designation.

High school accounting study is an important step to an accounting career. Students completing study using this textbook will have a broad background in *accounting principles*, skills, and concepts. The study will include day –to – day accounting tasks such as analyzing and recording financial information. Various typical accounting records are studied in chapters 2, 5, 6, 11, 12, 13, 20, 21, 22, and 23. Common activities in summarizing and reporting accounting information are studied in Chapter 7, 8, 14, 15, and 27. Specialized accounting functions are studied in chapter 10, 17, 15, 19, 22, 23, 24, 25, 26, 25, 29, and 30. The study includes common accounting concepts and procedure needed for entry level positions on the first there career ladder steps. The learning also is basic background for earning promotions and for continuing accounting study in college.

The accounting profession is guided by basic *accounting concepts*. The eleven concepts described in this chapter are commonly accepted by professional accounts. The material in this textbook illustrates the application of these concepts. Each time an application of a concept occurs, a concept reference is given.

Financial changes are reported for a specific period of time in the form of *financial statements*.

Accounting records are summarized periodically and reported to business owners or managers. The reports or statements are prepared for a specific period of time. The period of time may be one every month, every three months, every six months, or every year. Most individuals summarize personal financial information once every year in order to prepare tax reports.

Financial statements should contain all information necessary for a reader to understand a business' financial condition.

Helpful vocabulary:

high school	المدرسةالثانوية
broad background	خلفية واسعة
day-to-day accounting tasks	أعمال محاسبة يومية
financial information	معلومات مالية
accounting concepts	مفاهيم محاسبية
professional accountants	محاسبون مهنيون
accounting records	سجلات محاسبية
tax reports	تقارير ضريبية
accounting period cycle	دورة الفترة المحاسبية
financial condition	الوضع المالي
adequate disclosure	الإفصاح الكافي
business entity	كيان المؤسسة التجارية
current market price	سعر السوق الحالي
financial statement	بيان مالي
accounting period	فترة محاسبية
accounting principles	مبادئ محاسبية
lower value	القيمة الأدنى
consistent reporting	تقارير متَّسقة

Exercise 1. *Translate the previous passage into Arabic.*

Exercise 2. *Fill in this table with the suitable English derivatives whenever possible, and write down the Arabic equivalents of all the words.*

	Verb		Noun		Adjective	
English	Arabic	English	Arabic	English	Arabic	
start						
				complete		
		skill				
		concept				
				broad		
include						
act						
		step				
analyze						
learn						
earn						
		reference				
				specific		
study						
		month				
occur						
describe						

Exercise 3. *Translate these terms:*

passenger insurance	————	payment in full	————
passenger liner	————	payment on account	————
pay check	————	payment on delivery	————
payee	————	payment on receipt	————
payer	————	personal manager	————

191

UNIT 45

ACCOUNTING: AN
INFORMATIO
SYSTEM

Some companies, by the nature of their activities, are required to report periodically to certain *regulatory agencies*. For example, certain banks must report to the Comptroller of the Currency, and most public utility companies must report to a public utility commission. The regulatory agency may use the reported information to monitor solvency (as in the case of the banks) or the rate of income to be earned (as in the case of public utilities). Although these reports are based primarily on accounting data, often they must be prepared in accordance with additional conditions, rules and definitions. Some agencies, such as stock exchanges and the Securities and Exchange Commission, do require reports prepared in accordance with the generally accepted accounting principles that we shall discuss later. We have, therefore, shown certain regulatory agencies in both channels C and D of Exhibit 1-1.

One of the most important functions of the *accounting process* is to accumulate and report accounting information that shows an organization's financial position and the results of its operations. Many businesses publish such financial statements at least annually. The subdivision of the accounting process that produces these general-purpose reports is referred to as **financial accounting**. Financial accounting is essentially retrospective, because it deals primarily with historical information or events that have already happened. Its focus is on income determination and financial position as an aggregate financial picture of an enterprise.

Although *financial accounting data* are primarily historical, they are also useful for planning and control. Indeed, a considerable amount of planning must be based on what has happened in the recent past. In addition, historical financial information is inherently a control mechanism, since it can be used to measure the success of past planning. We should also emphasis that, although financial accounting is primarily historical, it is not merely a process of "filing in the numbers." As you study further, you will discover that determining the financial position and profitability of an enterprise is an exceedingly complex job that requires professional judgment.

Financial accounting statement are the main source of information for parties – other than governmental agencies – outside the business firm. Because these reports will often be used to evaluate management, their objectivity could be subject to question. To establish the validity of their *financial statements*, most firms have them audited by independent public accountants.

Helpful vocabulary:

by the nature of	يحكم بطبيعة
to report periodically	أنْ يُبْلغ دورياً
to monitor solvency	تراقَبَ القدرة على الدفع
based on accounting data	قائمة على البيانات محاسبية
stock exchanges	أسواق الأوراق المالية
final position	الوضع المالي
financial statements	بيانات مالية
financial accounting	محاسبة مالية
control mechanism	آلية ضبط
complex job	مهمة معقّد
professional judgment	رأي مهنيّ
subject to question	خاضع للسؤال
independent public accountant	محاسب عام مستقل
reservations about the statements	تحفّظات بشأن البيانات
free from bias	خالية من التحيُّز
business practices	الممارسات التجارية
formulation of accounting principle	صياغة المبادئ المحاسبية
regulatory bodies	هيئة منظّمة
conflict with	يتعرض مع
tax regulation	الأنظمة الضريبية
taxable income	الدخل الخاضع للضريبة
subject to examination by	خاضع للتدقيق من
managerial accounting	محاسبة إدارية

Exercise 1. *Translate the previous passage into Arabic.*

Exercise 2. *Fill in this table with the suitable English derivatives whenever possible, and write down the Arabic equivalents of all the words.*

Verb		Noun		Adjective	
English	Arabic	English	Arabic	English	Arabic
monitor					
		production			
report					
		objectivity			
accept					
				complex	
		validity			
focus					
				altered	
		auditor			
regulate					
				determined	
		bias			
discover					
				specified	
		guide			
profit					

Exercise 3. *Translate these terms:*

qualified endorsement	———————	rate war	———————
quantity rebate	———————	real cost	———————
quotations committee	———————	real estate market	———————
rate of exchange	———————	real estate tax	———————
rate of increase	———————	reduced prices	———————

Text Sources

Unit 1. Maheshwari, S. R. *Administrative Theories*. New Delhi: Allied
  Publishers Limited, 1994. (pp. 1-2).

Unit 2. Heady, F *Public Administration*: A comparative Perspective. New
  York: Marcel Dekker, INC, 1944. (PP.4-5).

Unit 3. Wolod, D. *The Study of Public Administration*. New York: Random
  House, 1997. (pp. 3 – 4).

Unit 4. Kuchhal, M.C. *Business Law*. New Delhi: Vikas Publishing Houle
  PVTLTD, 1996. (PP. 1.1 -1.2) .

Unit 5. Mercer, J. L. *Public Management Systems*: An Administrator's Guide.
  New York: Amacon, 1998 (pp.8-9).

Unit 6. Macra , S. *Public Administration* : An Introduction . New York :
  English Language Book Society , 1990. (pp .8 - 9).

Unit 7. Rothwell, K. J. *Administrative Issues in Developing Economies* .
  London : D. C. Heath and Company, 1992 . (pp. 3 - 4).

Unit 8. Gant, G .F. *Development Administration*. Wisconsin : The University
  of Wisconsin Press , 1999 . (pp. 3 – 4) .

Unit 9. Welch, S. *Quantitative Methods for Public Administration
  Technique and Applications. California* : Brooks / Cole
  Publishing company, 1993. (pp. 2-3).

Unit 10. Riggs, F .W. *Administration in Developing Countries*.
  Boston: Houghton Mifflin Company, 1994. (pp. 7-8).

Unit 11. Coventry, W. F. *Management Made Simple* . London: Howard and Wyndham Company, 1990 . (pp. 7-8) .

Unit 12. Craig, P. P. *Administrative Law*. London : Sweet and Maxwell, 1999. (pp .4-5) .

Unit 13. Kopelman, R. E. *Managing Productivity in Organizations*. New York: Mc Graw-Hill, 1996. (pp. 11-12).

Unit 14. Beck, E. F. *Basic Hospital Financial Management*. New York: Aspen Publishers. Inc, 1999. (pp. 1-2).

Unit 15. Vines, D. *Demand Management*. London: Gorge Allen and Unwin Publisher Ltd, 1993. (pp .26-27).

Unit 16. Neveu, R.D. *Fundamentals of Managerial Finance*. Dallas: South – Western Publishing Co , 1991 . (pp. 13- 14).

Unit 17.Narang, G. B. S. *Industrial and Works Management*. Delhi Khanna Publishers, 1997. (PP34-35).

Unit18. Narang, G.B, S. *Industrial and Works Management*. Delhi Khanna Publishers, 1997. (pp. 2-3)

Unit 19. Gupta, R. S. *Elements of Management*. New Delhi: Kalyani Publishers, 1997. (pp. 14 -15)

Unit 20. Plec, M. V. *Industrial Relations and Relations and Personnel Managemen*t . New Delhi : Vikas Publishing House PVT LTD, 1995. (PP. 3- 4).

Unit 21. Weston, J .F. *Essential of Management Finance*. New York: The Dryden press, 1997. (pp. 3-4).

Unit 22. Rao, S .B. *Financial Management*. New Delhi: Vikas Publishing Housing PVT LTD, 1994. (PP.30).

Unit 23. Herber , B. P. *Modern Public Finance* . Delhi All India Traveller Bookseller, 1998. (Pp.3-5).

Unit 24. Barber, M. P. *Public Administration*. London: Macdonald And Evans Ltd , 1993 .(pp. 25-26).

Unit 25. Union of Arab Banks. *Strategy of International Banking Business*. Tunis: NA, 1996. (pp. 20-21).

Unit 26. Harris , J. M *International Finance* . New York: Barron's Business Library, 1992. (pp 2-3).

Unit 27. Ibrahim, M. N. *Strategy of International Banking Business Banking Trading Programs*. Tunis: Union of Arab Banks.
1996. (pp 22 -23).

Unit 28. Pond , J. *Jonathan Pond's Guide to Investment and Finical planning* . New York : Institute of Finance, 1991. (pp 1-2).

Unit 29. Melvin, M. *International Money and Finance*. New York: Addision Wesley, Inc, 2000. (pp .28-29).

Unit 30. Passell, p. *The Money Manual*. New York: prentice-Hall Press, 1991.(pp 2-3) .

Unit 31. Shekhar, K.C. *Banking Theory and practice*. New Delhi: Vikas Publishing House PVT LTD , 1994 .(PP 199-200).

Unit 32. Eichberger, J. *Financial Economics*. London: Oxford University press, 1997. (pp 199-200).

Unit 33. Madura, J. *Financial Markets and Institutions*. New York: West Publishing Company, 1999. (pp. 4- 5).

Unit 34. Berry, A. *Bank Lending*. London : Chapman and Hall, 1993. (pp. 1-2).

Unit 35. Daff, T. *Quantitative and Accounting Methods*. New York: English language Book Society , 1993 .(pp . 1-2).

Unit 36. Harris, P .J. *Accounting and Finance for the International Hospital Industry* . Boston : Butterworth – Heinemann, 1995. (pp. 4- 5).

Unit 37. Hay, L. E. *Essentials of Accounting for Governmental and Not – for – profit Organizations.* Irwin: NA, 1997. (PP 1-2).

Unit 38. Short, D. G. *Fundamentals of Financial Accounting.* Boston: IRWIN ,Homewood , INC , 1990 .(pp . 4-5).

Unit 39. Vinnicombe, S. *The Essence of Women in Management.* New York: Pentice Hall , 1995 . (3- 5) .

Unit 40. Bauer, R. D. *Elementary Accounting.* New York: Barnes and Noble Books, 1993. (pp. 2-3).

Unit 41. Schroeder, R.G. *Accounting Theory.* New York: John Wiley and Sons, 1998 (pp. 1-2).

Unit 42. Gee, P. *Spicer and Pegler's Book – Keeping and Accounting.* New York : ELBS , 1998 . (PP .14 -15).

Unit 43 . Lowery, R .C. *Supervisory Management.* New Jersey: prentice-Hall, 1995. (pp . 5-7) .

Unit 44 . Swanson. R . M. *Accounting.* Chicago: South Western publishing Co , 1992. (pp.2-9).

Unit 45. Walgenbach, P. H . *Financial Accounting.* New York: Harcounrt Braces Jovanovich College Publishers, 1990. (pp 6-7).

Printed in the United States
By Bookmasters